Word of Life.

The House that God Built

The Story of Jack Wyrtzen By Harry Bollback

Unless otherwise noted, all Scripture quotations are taken from the New King James Version of the Holy Bible. Copyright ©1982 by Thomas Nelson, Inc. Used by permission. All rights reserved.

Copyright 1972 by
Word of Life Fellowship, Inc. Schroon Lake, New York 12870 Updated 1998, 2005, 2015

Printing History
November 1972 6,100 copies
February 1973 25,000 copies
June 1988 10,000 copies
March 1998 10,000 copies
June 2005 2,500 copies
March 2017 2,500 copies
November 2022 2,500 copies

ISBN: 978-0-692-80571-8

Printed in the United States of America

DEDICATION

*To those friends who through their support, prayers
and gifts have helped to build the house.*

FOREWORD

Once you begin, you won't be able to put this book down until you finish it. Engagingly written by one who has been associated with Word of Life for many years, this is the exciting account of what God did through the dedicated life of Jack Wyrtzen.

In these pages you will read of Jack's conversion, the struggles of his coming to a place of full dedication, his remarkable walk by faith, the opening up of the many facets of his ministry in evangelism, camp work, missionary outreach, radio, Bible clubs, concert ministries and the Bible Institute. But, most of all, your heart will be blessed as you read the stories of lives who have been changed by the grace of God.

As you read, you will find yourself asking, "What accounts for the blessing of God on the ministry of this man?" Surely his great vision, his unswerving loyalty to the Lord and His Word, his uncompromising stand on matters of doctrine and conduct, his determination to reach as many people as possible, and his hearty spirit of rejoicing are all part of the answer. But, basically, the answer is in the author's words, God "sought for a man, one to whom He could trust His work, and He found one."

One day while eating lunch with Jack, he was relating a story of how a certain person's life had challenged someone else. Then he commented, But, that's what we're all supposed to do, isn't it? Provoke one another unto love and good works. (Hebrews 10:24) Certainly Jack's life did. And may the story of his ministry do the same to all who read it.

Charles C. Ryrie, Ph.D.
Dallas, Texas

ACKNOWLEDGEMENTS

I met Jack Wyrtzen in 1941 and for 55 years we traveled, worked, preached, and prayed together. It is this firsthand knowledge of Jack and the ministry of Word of Life that gave me the background necessary for writing this book.

The first edition of The House that God Built was published in 1972 with the help of many people: Jack Wyrtzen and his family, who gave their fullest cooperation; Don "Robbie" Robertson; Forrest Forbes; Fred Scharmann; Al Kunz and Florence Otterbeck, who gave valuable insights on the early days of the ministry; George Sweeting, whose book, The Jack Wyrtzen Story, I used for reference; my wife, Mildred, who gave the help and encouragement necessary; Wylam Price, who helped with the editing and Linda Burton, who faithfully typed and retyped the manuscript.

In the first few years after The House that God Built was published, Jack literally received thousands of letters and comments from people who were inspired or ministered to by the book and wanted to hear more.

Sixteen years after it was published, the book underwent its first major revision. The update required considerable editing and the addition of new material. The task was accomplished with the help of several staff members, and it was decided that references to my name would be rendered in the third person so as not to disrupt the flow of the narrative. With the Homegoing of Jack in 1996 and the continued expansion of the work of Word of Life around the world, we found it necessary in 1998 to once again update the book as the story of changed lives continued to be used by God to encourage believers.

In 2005 I made another update on the history of Word of Life, and I wrote, "This is probably the last time that I will have the privilege of updating this book." But, here I am in 2016 adding a few more chapters to the history of Word of Life. I think I can say with certainty that this will be my last. The wonderful part of this story is that the worldwide ministry of Word of Life continues to move ahead for the glory of God.

If the Lord tarries, there will be more editions that others will write, but it has been my joy to be a part of Word of Life for 75 years. Praise the Lord for the great and godly leadership of Word of Life through the years, and may they continue to stand strong for the Lord as they "Hold Forth the Word of Life."

In 2021, Harry Bollback went home to be with the Lord. Two additional chapters, (19 and 20) have been added to this book sharing updates since the book was last published.

PREFACE

Perhaps the whole story of Word of Life can be summed up in one word – miracles. Jack Wyrtzen is proof that God is still a miracle-working God and that He continues to use men to accomplish His program. Word of Life is a story of a man who was used of God.

Many times when Jack preached, he talked about ministries that began, grew and then disappeared from the scene. Jack often said, "First, there is a man, then a movement and then a monument."

This book is not a monument to Jack Wyrtzen (that's the last thing Jack would want), but it is the story of how God is using Word of Life in the twenty-first century to reach people around the world with the Gospel. I have not tried to write a complete history of Word of Life, but rather the story of a man who made himself completely available to God. My purpose is to show how God could use any of us to do similar things for His glory, for all of us are building something – either good or bad. It's either for the glory of God or not. We only live once. Someone put it this way:

> *Only one life, 'twill soon be past;*
> *Only what's done for Christ will last.*

Jack lived Jeremiah 33:3, Call unto me, and I will answer thee, and show thee great and mighty things, which thou knowest not.

Harry Bollback
Schroon Lake, New York

TABLE OF CONTENTS

Foreword
Acknowledgements
Preface

1. The Entrance Gate 11
2. The Foundation 17
3. The Frame 25
4. The Building 31
5. The Family Room 39
6. The Wiring 55
7. The Attic 63
8. The Landscaping 71
9. The Windows 81
10. The Yard 93
11. The Guest Room 97
12. The Plumbing 103
13. The Study 111
14. The Roof 123
15. Phase 1: Construction Completed 131
16. New Owners 137
17. Até Logo (Until we meet again) 143
18. Remodeling 151
19. Another Goodbye 157
20. Changes and New Plans... 161

CHAPTER 1

The Entrance Gate

Behold, I stand at the door and knock...
Revelation 3:20

I thought I was Jesus Christ and my girlfriend an incarnation of the devil. Where, oh, where was God? Then one day I found Him on the Island of Love.

When I was seven years old, I moved to New York City from Greece. It wasn't easy because I couldn't speak English, and I didn't have many friends. The other kids would always let the air out of my bicycle tires. I tried to be kind to them, but I didn't know how to be their friend. I wanted to be a good person, but I didn't know how to do that either. There were many things I wanted to do and many people I wanted to get to know, but how?

One of the things I wanted to do was learn to play a guitar. I remember my first guitar; I made it myself with rubber bands and a box. I did learn to play, and soon I was playing pretty well. From there things started to move fast. I was playing well enough to be a part of a group. We played rock and roll music, and I was living among people who thought as I did. By this time, I had a girlfriend; I was high on sex and drugs. One night around 3:00 a.m. when I took her home, I said, "good night", and then I tried to convince her to come and live with me. She hesitated at the door; I knew she didn't want to face her mother the next day.

I said, "Vicky, you know your Mom and Dad will go through the same routine tomorrow morning. They will want to know why you are running around with a wild guy like me. They say they love you, but what do they know about love? They really only care about what the neighbors are saying." She left me.

My name is Tasos Mahairas. At that time, I was an 18-year-old high school dropout on pot. I was on pot because I wanted to know God. I wanted to become God-conscious, and the pot helped me to meditate. I thought it made me sensitive to other people and their emotions. I could tell if someone was a hypocrite while I was still able to overlook myself.

Eventually, Vicky was forced out of her home, and she came to live with me and some others who shared our lifestyle. We shared a four-room apartment with Kurt and Tanya. We had very little money and no possessions. We slept on a mattress on the floor. That was all we wanted.

One day we tried LSD, and, for some reason, it made us think about God. I was a Greek Orthodox, and Vicky was Roman Catholic. We had both given up formal religion because we thought it was all fake.

I began to meditate, look at the sun, and walk through Central Park. Soon I had strange dreams and woke up believing I was Jesus Christ.

We planned a trip to California. We were going to hitchhike, but the night before we were to leave, all of us except Vicky went on another drug trip. Tanya went berserk; she blew her mind. She kept saying, "Life's a game; it's all a game." One would think that the rest of us would never want to try it again, but it wasn't that easy and we had another trip. It was a bad one. I was now convinced I was Jesus Christ and that Vicky was the devil trying to trick me.

So, in July 1968, I left her and New York City and went north looking for God. I was walking along the beach in Lake George, dirty and unkempt and not even caring, when a young man stopped me and asked me a few questions. I thought he, just like Vicky, was the devil trying to trick me.

He told me about a beautiful Island on Schroon Lake and that he would pay for me to spend a week there. Even though it sounded good to me, I thought I was dreaming or on a delayed drug trip.

We took a boat over to the Island. Once when I was a kid, I had a dream that I had gone to an island where everybody loved each other; they were singing, and everybody was happy. Now here I was in the back seat of a powerful speedboat, and when the boat took off, all I could see was sky. I remembered my dream. Was I on the way to the island that was in my dream? Was I on the way to my Island of Love?

In just a few moments I was there. I noticed that this Island was a beautiful place. Everybody was kind; everybody was singing. They accepted me, and nobody made fun of me.

This was what I was looking for. A man stood up and told me about a wonderful friend called Jesus. Suddenly I realized how wrong I had been. I had never been Jesus Christ! This man told me my life could be changed if I would but receive the Heaven-sent Jesus Christ as my Savior. Then this preacher spoke to me alone, and I made that all-important decision to trust in Jesus.

Where was I?

Word of Life Island

Who was that man? Jack Wyrtzen

The next day I phoned Vicky and said, "Vicky, I think I have found what we have been looking for."

"What is it?"

"I found God."

She said, "You know, I think I know what you're talking about." "How can you?" I asked.

"Yesterday, I was at a beach here in New York, and a young man asked me some questions about God and gave me a book about some saints."

I said, "What saint is it?"

"Hold on, I'll get the book; I'll find out." In a moment she was back. She said, "The book is St. John."

"That's the one, Vicky, that's the one! Come on up. I'll tell you more." "I don't have any money."

I turned to my new friend, Jack Wyrtzen. "Don't worry about that," he said, "Just get her here."

So, Vicky came to the Island, and I began to tell her about Jesus. Then I introduced her to my friend, and he spoke to her. She also received the Lord Jesus Christ as her Savior. Later, Jack Wyrtzen married us.

Update

Tom Mahairas started a Bible study in his home which in 1974 grew into Manhattan Bible Church. Tom was the Pastor for many years and is still an active Elder there and preaches there often. Tom was also the founder of Manhattan Christian Academy, Transformation Life Center, New York GO, The Love Kitchen, and in 1996 he founded CitiVision. As the Founding President of CitiVision, Tom travels to churches, schools, prisons, and events sharing his passion and vision for seeing lives transformed by the power of the Gospel.

I was home in Kearny, New Jersey, where all the local political leaders were gathered to discuss the possibility of my running for the office of mayor. Everybody was waiting for my answer in the smoke-filled room. The haze from the cigars seemed to hang motionless in the room.

What should I do? A little while before, my wife had left me, feeling she could no longer stand my way of life. Just then the telephone rang, and I jumped up to answer it thinking it might be my wife, but it wasn't. It was my granddaughter, Judy. She was inviting me to go with her to a Word of Life Rally at the Mosque Theater in Newark. It was hard to refuse her – she was somebody special in my life, and I usually did whatever she wanted. But why a religious rally? I had enough religion all my life.

"No, Judy, I can't make it tonight."

She was disappointed and hung up. I thought, "After all, I am Walter Oliver, a candidate for mayor of Kearny." I was definitely on my way up in politics, perhaps even to the governorship of New Jersey. I was in much demand as a speaker and toastmaster, especially at men's meetings. The phone rang a second time. My granddaughter, Judy, begged me to go to the rally. I thought, "Well, a little religion won't hurt anyone – not even a politician."

That night in the Mosque Theater I got more than I had bargained for. The crowd was singing:

> *Just as I am, without one plea*
> *But that Thy blood was shed for me,*
> *And that Thou bidd'st me come to Thee,*
> *O Lamb of God, I come, I come!*

There I sat, staring – a hard-boiled politician glued to my seat.

The speaker said, "You've been living for the devil long enough. Why don't you start living for God?" My granddaughter turned to me and said, "I'll go down with you, Gramps, if you're afraid to stand up and go by yourself." You know, that was more than I could take. Believe me, I could stand rough-and-tough politics without batting an eye, but when I stood to my feet with my little granddaughter, tears started rolling down my cheeks. I gave my heart to the Lord Jesus Christ. Old things dropped away.

Later, at a political meeting, I announced that I was out of the mayoral race because I had a personal experience with Jesus Christ.

So, Walter Oliver came to the Lord. He was born again. Where did this happen?

At a Word of Life Rally!

And who was the man giving the invitation to come and receive Christ? Jack Wyrtzen!

Just as Tasos Mahairas and Walter Oliver were without hope before they met Jesus, every man or woman who has not met Jesus is without hope. But just as God made a way back for Adam and Eve when they sinned, God's love and grace has made a way back for all who put their faith and trust in Jesus.

The love of God was demonstrated through Jesus when He was here by the way He loved people; always looking for ways to meet their needs and to deal tenderly with sinners. The first person He appeared to after His resurrection was Mary Magdalene. She had experienced the transforming power of God in her life when Jesus cast out her demons. God's matchless power transforms man at his worst. It is that same power of God that has been at work through the ministries of Word of Life.

Thousands of men and women and boys and girls have experienced freedom from the power of sin in their lives after attending a Word of Life Rally or Camp. Many have come to know Jesus through the radio and TV programs. Then these transformed people have returned to their place in society changed by the power of God. Many of them have become full-time evangelists or missionaries. Others have developed into leaders at their churches or rescue missions. Some have trained to be Bible Club leaders or Christian camp workers. The power of God is still at work transforming lives around the world.

CHAPTER 2

The Foundation

For no other foundation can anyone lay than that which is laid, which is Jesus Christ. I Corinthians 3:11

"Hey George, get down from that flagpole!" It was about 2:00 a.m. at the United States army base. George Schilling had been out for a blast with two of the boys. He was now pretty "high" and had climbed to the top of the flagpole and wouldn't come down. If there ever was a confused, mixed-up person in the 101st Cavalry Band in Brooklyn, it was George Schilling. He was looking for meaning in life but hadn't found it.

One day that changed, and everyone in the 101st Cavalry Band was shocked when George Schilling showed up with a Bible and Gospels of John. George handed them out to everyone because he had finally found the meaning of life. He had discovered God through Jesus Christ. "You're the last guy I'd ever expect to see with a Bible," Jack said to George.

Jack Wyrtzen along with the other young men in the band thought they were pretty good. Jack had quite a bit of religion in those days. He wasn't a fanatic, but he went to church on Easter and Christmas.

All the men refused the Gospels including Jack Wyrtzen. They assured George they were not the least bit interested in reading it. George was insistent, and finally Jack took one just to be polite. He stuffed it in his back pocket and forgot all about it.

That night as Jack stood at the railroad station, he put his hands in his pocket and discovered the book. He took it out and read the cover, "The Gospel of Saint John". In Jack's mind, it wouldn't have been bad if it had just said, "The Gospel of John", but the "Saint" business was just too much. That was simply too much religion for anybody. Jack tore the book into pieces and threw it off the train platform.

A few days later George met up with Jack and asked, "How are you getting along with the "Gospel of John" I gave you last week?"

Jack responded, "Gospel of John? What Gospel? Oh, do you mean that little book with Saint John on the cover?"

"Yes, have you read it?"

"Read it? Listen George, I threw it away before I even got home," Jack answered.

"You did?" he said. "Here's another one." George was persistent in his witness to Jack and kept giving him tracts and Gospels.

Soon it was time for the National Guard camp again. Everyone remembered how George had climbed to the top of the flagpole the year before. They all wondered if George's newfound religion would affect his behavior this year. This would be a test. Taps sounded... lights out... and, all of a sudden, a little light came on, and George began reading the Bible with his flashlight. The fellows cursed him, threw shoes at him and anything else they could find. But he stayed with it. He was a man.

Jack watched George at the army camp for two full weeks. He noticed a complete change in George's life. He wasn't sure what George had that made him different, but Jack wanted it, too. It didn't take Jack long to discover what it was and to make it his also. (That directness actually became a lifelong characteristic of Jack. It wasn't that he was an opportunist; it was that God had gifted him with discernment to know what the next thing was God wanted him to do, and God would always help him find a way to do it.)

Jack attended a church meeting with George but had angrily walked out because the preacher's words upset him. That night in the darkness of his room, Jack began to ponder his own life and wondered why a sermon from a little preacher who really didn't even know what life was all about should upset him.

Jack's life seemed to be going well. He was young and on the move. He was busy directing his own dance band; he had a good job in the insurance business; he was playing in the United States Cavalry band, and he was keeping company with a society girl. Besides all that, Jack reasoned, he did have some religion. He could remember when he was a little kid in the Unitarian Sunday School singing, "Jesus loves me, this I know". Then he became a Methodist, a Presbyterian, and now he was going to a Baptist church.

Why be upset? Why should he let a little sermon bother him?

All of a sudden, Jack remembered the words of a Bible-believing pastor who had been in the Wyrtzen home a little while before. After the pastor had talked with Jack about the Lord Jesus, Jack had asked, "Well, suppose I don't believe any of this stuff that you're telling me?"

The pastor answered, "You'll be lost forever."

As he lay there on his bed in the darkness of his room, those words kept repeating in Jack's mind. "Lost forever, lost forever, lost forever." What was happening? He imagined eternity without God and without hope. He realized for the first time that even though he was religious, he was a sinner, and he needed Jesus Christ, God's Son. He slipped out of bed and got down on his knees and admitted to God that his life was ruined by sin. He asked Jesus Christ to save him. He was saved! No question about it. Old things passed away and all things became new.

But how could he ever tell his girlfriend, Marge Smith, about Jesus Christ? Jack didn't want to lose her, so he decided to play it cool and not mention his decision to her.

In the meantime, Marge's mother had grown concerned about her daughter. Mrs. Smith was a Christian, and although she had no real desire to live for the Lord or to separate herself from the things of the world, she was worried about her daughter keeping company with a dance band leader. That wasn't what she had in mind for her daughter's future.

Mrs. Smith had listened to a radio program called, The Young People's Church of the Air. The speaker was Percy Crawford. She found the program very interesting as she had never heard young people talk in such a personal way about Christ before. She tried to encourage Jack and Marge to listen to Percy Crawford's program.

Jack and Marge didn't want to hear Percy Crawford and made sure they never made it home on time. However, frequently something would happen, and Jack and Marge would arrive home in time to hear the close of the program.

"Jack," Marge said, "hearing Percy speak does something to me. But I'll throw it off like most people do. It makes me feel uneasy when I hear it, but I'll forget it."

When summer came, Mrs. Smith announced to Marge that they were going to take their brand-new car and head off on a vacation. Marge would get to be the chauffeur. This was exciting news, and since Marge thought that they were heading to the exclusive Pocono Manor, she packed for the occasion, including all her evening gowns. Soon they were packed and headed off to the Pocono Mountains.

When they passed through Stroudsburg, Marge's mother said, "You'd better pull over here; I have something to tell you." Marge pulled the car over and her mother continued, "We're not going to the Pocono Manor. We're going to Pinebrook Bible Camp."

"Is that the man you listen to on the radio each Sunday – The Young People's Church of the Air? Percy Crawford?", Marge asked.

"That's right," Mrs. Smith answered.

"Forget it!" Marge answered. "Count me out. You'll never get me into a place like that." So, she turned the car around and started back home.

It took her mother quite a while before she convinced Marge she needed to turn back around and head to Pinebrook. Actually, they were halfway home when she said, "Marge, would you just do it for my sake?" In order to please her mother, Marge finally decided she would go to the camp but only stay one night. After that, she would leave.

As soon as they arrived, Marge knew this was not the place for her. Just an hour before they arrived, the cook had quit, and now if they wanted dinner they would have to drive back to town. Being a good-natured soul with plenty of money, Marge invited all the other kids to go, too. So, they drove off in their cars and ate at Marge's expense.

When they arrived back at camp, Mrs. Smith said, "I want you to meet Mr. Crawford."

"Forget it, I don't want to meet him." Marge walked away and left her mother standing there.

In spite of everything, Marge actually decided her first night at Pinebrook wasn't too bad. There was a lot of good music which she enjoyed. There was a quartet who sang, and they seemed excited and on fire for God. This was unusual for Marge as these men surely seemed different from the fellows whom she usually spent time with. They surely didn't look like the young men who played in Jack's band. There wasn't any preaching that night either which made Marge happy.

Later that night when Marge finally met Percy Crawford, he said, "Tomorrow morning when I preach, if you don't accept the Lord, I don't want you to stay any longer. I know you are having a good time, but I don't want you hardening your heart to the Lord. That is dangerous!"

Tuesday morning came, and Percy gave his message. Marge thought for sure that somebody had told him all about her. It appeared like he pointed his finger and shouted at her through the whole message. Percy had a special way of giving the invitation, and when he finished his sermon, he invited people to come and receive the Lord. It was hard for Marge to resist his sincere invitation. Marge decided she'd raise her hand; she'd do that much, but she wouldn't walk forward.

Marge looked around and saw a little boy walking to the front. But as she watched the little boy she thought, "If that little kid has enough courage to do it, what's wrong with me?"

She stood to her feet and walked forward. Twenty other young people came forward to receive the Lord as Savior. Some were emotional and crying, but Marge stood there 'like a sphinx'. Everybody in the camp was thrilled that Marge or the "Fifth Avenue Belle", as some had come to call her, had gone forward.

When the meeting was over, Percy came and shook Marge's hand. Because Marge didn't feel different and she wasn't crying or emotionally upset, she said, "Well, Percy, I guess I'm not saved."

"I know you're saved. You're going to do great things for God. He's going to use you," Percy answered.

"How dumb can this man be?" Marge thought to herself. She didn't feel saved. Could she be saved?

Marge returned to her room, closed the door, and fell on her bed and cried. She began to realize the full impact of what it meant to confess her sins to Jesus and to make a public profession of that decision.

Marge's mother came into the room. "Marge," she said, "I want you to write a letter to your boyfriend and tell him that you received the Lord as your Savior and that now you're a Christian. Tell him you're not interested in getting married to a dance band leader."

Mrs. Smith insisted that Marge write the letter because she did not want her daughter to be involved in the kind of life lived by Jack Wyrtzen. She hoped the letter would put an end to the relationship and that Marge would forget Jack and move on with her life.

Jack still hadn't told Marge that he had made a decision to receive Jesus Christ into his heart. Marge finally got the courage to write him, and along with her letter she sent him a tract called, "How to be Saved". In the letter she said, "Honey, I am saved, and I want you to be saved. But don't get saved until I get home because I want to save you. Marge" A few days later a telegram arrived at Pinebrook.

Percy Crawford's camp was certainly known for being fun, and anyone who had ever been there would come home raving about the fun and excitement that took place in the dining room. Percy would make everyone who received a letter or telegram stand on a stool in the dining room and read their mail out loud.

Now it was Marge's turn to get on the stool. Marge got up and read, "Dear Marge, Praise the Lord! I have been saved for the last few months, but I've been afraid to tell you. I'm so thankful that the Lord has saved you. Jack"

Everyone clapped and cheered because they'd all been praying for this dance band leader. It was quite a surprise to discover that he was already saved. Marge stood on the stool, crying, while everybody was clapping.

Percy turned to her and said, "What are you crying for?"

"I'm crying because I didn't save him. I wanted to get home and save Jack. I didn't want anybody else to save him." Marge answered.

Things had certainly changed for Marge.

Pinebrook had turned out to be a great place; it was the place where she found the Savior, and it was the place where she learned that her boyfriend, Jack, was a Christian. So, instead of staying just one day, Marge ended up staying two weeks. Marge cleaned tables and worked harder than she ever had before. Everybody at camp was really surprised to see this "Fifth Avenue Belle" working so hard.

In retrospect, Marge always said, "I loved the work I did at Pinebrook; it showed people that when you're in Christ you are a new creature."

Actually, in God's plan, all of this was preparation for another camp that Jack and Marge would one day open – a camp that would encircle the whole world. Nothing "just happens" in the life of a believer. God puts us in circumstances and in situations not to hinder us, not to give us a hard time, but to prepare us for the work He has for us to do and the perfect plan He has for our lives.

CHAPTER 3

The Frame

Lest it may happen, after he hath laid the foundation and is not able to finish it, all who behold it begin to mock him. Luke 14:29

As Jack and Marge began to pray and read the Bible together, they were convinced there was more to Christianity than just making a decision to receive Jesus as Savior. The struggle started when they began to understand what consecration meant according to God's Word.

Were they ready to unreservedly dedicate their lives to the Lord? Were they willing to lay their lives on the altar and truly say, "Lord, here am I, send me?" Through Bible study and the personal testimony of godly people, it soon became very clear that the people God chose to use were those who are fully surrendered to do the will of God.

For some people that decision is almost instantaneous at the time of their salvation. For others, the surrender can be a struggle. It wasn't easy for Jack. For a year he tried to serve two masters. He knew he should serve the Lord, but it was hard for him to make a clean break from his previous lifestyle.

In October 1933, Jack and Marge went back to Pinebrook for a special camp reunion. It was there that Jack met Stanley Kline, who later became a missionary to Africa. Jack and Stanley were assigned to be roommates for the weekend. Stanley was a dedicated, consecrated Christian man seeking to do God's will; Jack was still searching. Stanley's interests were in the things of God, reading the Word and praying. Because Jack was afraid Stanley would ask him questions or put him on the spot, Jack managed to steer clear of him for most of the weekend. Jack tried to avoid talking to Stanley during his devotional time, so he would go to bed either earlier or later than Stanley.

One night, however, they did have a conversation, so Jack asked Stanley, "Do you think it's alright for a Christian to play in a dance band and live for the Lord, too?"

Stanley, a dedicated Christian, tactfully and wisely turned to the Word of God and said, "Read this." It was Colossians 3:17, *And whatsoever you do in word or deed, do all in the name of the Lord Jesus, giving thanks to God and the Father by Him.*

"Jack," said Stanley, "if you, as a Christian, can play in the band and do it in the name of the Lord Jesus Christ and be happy, then it's one thing; if you cannot, then you had better quit."

Little did Stanley realize the impact those words would make on Jack Wyrtzen's life or how many times Jack would use those same verses in future years to show young people the answer concerning the questions they were facing in their own lives.

Jack and Marge were Christians, but they had yet to fully dedicate themselves to the Lord. They hadn't yielded their bodies to the Lord. They were saved, but that was all.

The next summer they went back to Pinebrook for another vacation. Albert Hughes was the speaker, and he challenged the young people to "go all out for God". Marge knew that because of her poor health she would never be able to go to the mission field, but as soon as Jack heard the challenge, his hand went right up. He was ready to go. He was a candidate for the mission field. Marge sat in her seat and thought, "Well, there goes our wedding plans, because I'm not going to the mission field."

Jack looked over at Marge and could see that she was upset so he put his hand back down. The speaker, Albert Hughes, came and spoke personally to them and said, "Jack, I want you to know that if you mean business and if you're dedicating your life to the Lord, it might mean breaking up with Marge." He paused and then continued, "However, it could mean if Marge would dedicate her life to the Lord along with you that God could completely change your lives so that you could both do something for the Lord."

The congregation was singing, "Where He Leads Me, I Will Follow"; they kept singing it and singing it. Jack sat in his seat praying. Marge was also talking to God. "Lord, when I said that I wanted to become a Christian, did it also mean that I had to sacrifice everything? Do I have to give up everything? Do I have to change all my plans?" Marge looked at Jack. He was praying, and the congregation was still singing. She hesitated.

"Jack, I'll stand with you. I'll surrender all to the Lord. I'll even go with you to the mission field. If need be, I'm ready to lay down my life for the Lord."

With the crowd still singing, "Where He Leads Me, I Will Follow", Jack and Marge stood up and dedicated their lives to the Lord. By this they were saying, "Lord, we are ready to do anything, willing to go any place, say anything, be anything and do anything for Your honor and glory." Both Jack and Marge felt they would soon be on the mission field. Some might think that now it would be easy for Jack to give up his dance band. On December 3rd, Jack's band was scheduled to play for a dance at the Hotel Ambassador on Park Avenue in New York City. Earlier in the day, Jack and Marge had attended the Army vs. Navy football game and had discussed the subject of a life fully surrendered to the will of God. By the time Jack left Marge to head to his job, he realized he was trying to straddle the fence. The Lord was pulling one way, and the world was pulling another.

Jack put on his tuxedo, grabbed his trombone and within a few minutes was seated on the subway headed to New York. Jack reasoned that the Lord would certainly understand what he was trying to do. Since Jack always carried tracts and Gospels of John in his pocket, he decided to give them out. There he was walking up and down the train, trombone under his arm, giving out tracts and telling people about his Savior.

He was late, but finally he arrived at the Hotel Ambassador. He looked in. The band was already playing, but for some reason he didn't have any desire to go in there with that crowd again. He stepped back out to the sidewalk and decided instead to get his shoes shined. As the boy shined his shoes, Jack told him about Jesus Christ, and when he left, he gave the boy a Gospel of John.

A struggle was going on, a tremendous conflict. When he had dedicated his life to the Lord, had he really meant everything? Was he willing to give up the dance band?

At that point, the band had started without him, but Jack felt that he had no choice but to go in and play for the rest of the dance. Around 1:00 a.m., the girl who had hired him for the event asked, "Jack, is everything alright? You're not acting like yourself tonight. Is something wrong?" Jack thought, "If you only knew!" Physically he felt fine, but spiritually he felt like a sick man.

When the dance was over, Jack met up with a young man from the liberal Baptist church he'd been attending. The young man said, "Jack, had you heard that my brother was killed in a car accident? He was coming home from a dance about two weeks ago when he was involved in a head-on collision. His body was cut right in two. He died instantly." The friend then volunteered to drive Jack home. On the way home, Jack began to share the plan of salvation. His friend listened and then turned to Jack and said, "I don't understand it; if you knew how to get to Heaven and about a place called Hell, how come you never told us?" He looked at Jack and said, "If my brother had known and believed, he would be in Heaven, but he probably didn't believe which means he's in Hell right now because you never told us!"

When Jack got back to his room, he fell on his knees and wrestled with God the whole night. At 5:00 a.m., still on his knees in his room, he told the Lord he was through with all the things that did not please Him. He also committed that he would use whatever skills God gave him to tell people about a real place called Heaven and a real place called Hell.

The next morning, December 4, 1933, Stanley Kline received a telegram. "Praise the Lord, dance band finished. Signed, Jack"

The foundation was laid; the frame was up. Now it was time for the building.

CHAPTER 4

The Building

...having been built on the foundation of the apostles and prophets, Jesus Christ Himself being the chief cornerstone, in whom the whole building, being fitted together, grows into a holy temple in the Lord... Ephesians 2:20-21

If the first nineteen years of Jack Wyrtzen's life had been useless to God, he was determined that the remaining years would be the opposite.

Jack was a man of great vision. He was also a very practical man. He worked hard; he was polite, always enthusiastic, tremendously optimistic, insistent, and courageous. He had an explicit and complete trust in his Lord and constantly expected God to do the impossible.

It all began on Monday nights when Jack got a small group of men together who were interested in studying the Bible. He started with two or three, and it grew until finally there were twenty-one in his bedroom every week. They didn't know who to go to for help in studying the Bible, but the Lord directed them to men like J. Arthur Reed and Alfred Kunz who taught them the true value of prayer and that they should expect God to teach them something new each day. That group was really the beginning of Word of Life, a little group called Chi Beta Alpha. Since the very inception of Word of Life, the work has been built on a book – the Bible.

The group grew and soon they needed a larger room for their meetings. Mrs. Wyrtzen, Jack's mother, who was always involved in politics, arranged for them to have a room at the Republican Headquarters for their weekly meetings. For four years Al Kunz taught their class and instructed the young men in the great doctrines of the Scriptures, great words in the Bible, and the Hebrew names of God.

Then Pastor Hermann Braunlin of the Hawthorne Gospel Tabernacle, along with Al Kunz and J. Arthur Springer, started a Monday night school that was called the Hawthorne Evening Bible School.

For the next four years, two or three carloads of young people from New York traveled to New Jersey to study the Word of God at the Hawthorne Evening Bible School. Even that was not enough for the men of Chi Beta Alpha. They also met every Tuesday night at the home of Al Kunz. In a very personal way, he taught them how to prepare sermons and deliver the Gospel message. Is it any wonder that so many of them caught the vision of getting the job done for God?

Mr. Kunz said of this small group, "I shall always be grateful to God for the privilege of being associated with such an earnest and dedicated group of godly young people who were so interested and intent on learning of God and working in all His ways." Besides Jack, the original group included Anne Lubkemann; Ray Studley; Fred Scharmann, who for many years was the business manager for Word of Life; Ernie Lubkemann, one of the young people saved at the first Word of Life banquet and who later became a missionary traveling all around the world with the Pocket Testament League; Bill Wiley who went on to become the home secretary of the South American Mission (formerly the South American Indian Mission); John Duchardt, who served as a pastor for many years with his wife, Bunny; Sophie Muller, a missionary who trekked through the jungles of South America reaching thousands of Indians with the Gospel.

Although Jack Wyrtzen's schedule became so busy with ministry meetings that he was not able to finish the three-year Bible course at Hawthorne, he was invited to give the first commencement address, and he was awarded an honorary diploma.

Through the years, Word of Life has always been a fellowship of God's people working together, praying together, and studying the Word together. Originally, George Schilling was the president, and Jack was the vice-president, but that changed when Jack was elected the president. After Jack became the president, there were no further elections. Jack was God's man for Word of Life, and no one ever bothered to bring the question up again. Through faith and prayer, the work grew under Jack's ministry.

A Council of Christians, mostly laypeople, was formed to help the ministry of Word of Life. Jack always sought the counsel and the prayers of other Christians. Although he earnestly sought the advice of others, he had a mind of his own. Even when many suggested he not do a particular thing, often after much prayer, he still went ahead and did it. He was usually right.

One day Jack approached Al Kunz, who by now was a member of the Council of Word of Life, and said, "I feel that with all the meetings we're having, the Lord is saying that I should quit my job and go full time. What do you think?"

Al Kunz, being a real man of God, thought for a minute and said, "Jack, don't do it if you can possibly help it. But if you have to, go ahead. Remember that you are already having a fruitful ministry."

Jack kept this sound advice in mind. He also kept praying about it. Meanwhile, the ministry of Word of Life began to take shape. The work of Word of Life has always been bold and often unorthodox. The Fellowship has one purpose and goal in mind – to lead men and women to a saving knowledge of Jesus Christ. Although never compromising in doctrine, Christian living, or co-operation, Word of Life always looks for something new... something different.

So, in May of 1934, the original group felt they ought to have a banquet. A requirement for admission included the unique idea that each person had to bring an unsaved friend and 75 cents for the meal.

Anne Lubkemann, who was such a tremendous blessing to the ministry in its early days, had shared the Gospel many times with her unsaved brother, Ernie. He was never interested in attending any meetings, but when she invited him to the banquet, he was interested. Ernie Lubkemann was saved that night, and later he and his wife, Leona, went into full-time service for the Lord.

One real problem for the Word of Life meetings was deciding who would do the preaching. There was Ray Studley, George Schilling, Henry Hutchinson and Jack Wyrtzen. Each man had one sermon. Since they had no way of deciding who would do the preaching, they usually flipped a coin, and the winner had the opportunity of preaching.

Another problem was deciding where to hold the meetings. Once after determining there were no local churches teaching the Word of God in their hometown, they decided to rent a church and have their own Sunday night evangelistic meeting. They looked around for the largest church they could find, and before they had even rented it, they had visions of it being full with many people accepting the Lord! But how could they get the auditorium?

Jack Wyrtzen was chosen as the man to go see the deacons of the church. Jack stood with great fear and trembling before the crowd of deacons in a smoke-filled room wondering how their request would ever get approved. Outside, the rest of Jack's friends were praying and claiming the promise that "the heart of the king is in the hands of the Lord."

One of the deacons turned to Jack and said, "Sonny, what do you want?"

Jack said, "We'd like to use your church auditorium for meetings."

The deacons asked Jack to wait outside while they made their decision. When they finally summoned Jack back into the room, they said, "We've decided not to give you the auditorium, but we'll allow you to use the large Sunday School room for October, November and December."

Jack rushed out to tell the others. They were thrilled. Already their vision was beginning to materialize. They went from house to house, ringing doorbells and inviting people to come to the meeting that Sunday night. At their first meeting George Schilling was the song leader and Jack was the preacher. Jack preached the Gospel message to over 200 people that first night and then gave an invitation. He was such a novice that he didn't know what to do when twenty-one people raised their hands for salvation. He dismissed them without even a word of prayer and just said, "Good night, everybody!"

The meetings began to grow. Interest was mounting, and on the fourth Sunday more than 400 people jammed into the auditorium. Now they were in trouble. Each of the guys had already preached their one and only sermon. They began calling up friends, and some of them came to help. At the conclusion of their three-month series, there were 625 people packed into the auditorium, and that night alone 55 put their faith in Jesus Christ.

One of Jack's next ideas was to form a Gospel team that traveled around visiting the Civilian Conservation Corps, commonly known as the CCC. This work was done under the auspices of the Pocket Testament League. During the summer, on vacations and at lunchtimes, they were constantly holding meetings. When they first started, they had an open-air meeting once a week. Then it was three times a week. Soon they were working on the streets seven nights a week. Before summer came, they set a goal to hold a street meeting in every town on Long Island.

Again, Jack began to wonder. Should he quit his job? Should he leave the insurance business? Should he go full time? Could he trust God completely? Mr. Kunz had told him when he couldn't keep up with both, then it would be time to quit his job and go full time for the Lord. Was this the time?

Soon the team was busily engaged in street meetings all over Long Island. Nobody had ever told them they needed permission to have street meetings. They were just so zealous for God they used every moment they had to tell the Good News.

One night in Huntington, Long Island, there was a large crowd standing around listening to the preaching. The crowd continued to grow until it spilled out into the street and stopped the traffic. People were blowing their horns, and everybody was excited. A policeman came to see what was going on. He was very annoyed with all the confusion in the street, so he dragged Jack and the Gospel team right in before the judge.

"Judge," he said, "these men are upsetting the whole town. They stopped the traffic on Main Street, right in front of the bank, and people were standing all over the sidewalks and out into the streets, causing an awful lot of confusion."

The judge looked at Jack and said, "What were you doing out there?" Jack described to the judge that they were telling people about Jesus Christ because they needed to be born again. As the judge listened to the testimony of these young people, instead of getting upset, he began to nod his head and soon he was smiling. He turned to the policeman and said, "Officer, take these men back to town. I want you to get some wooden horses and block off the whole street so these men can have their street meeting. I know what these men are talking about because I know the same Savior that they do. I know a lot about this town, and I know the people of this town need to know the Gospel. You'd better take good care of them." Then he added, "I'll be down in just a few moments. I'm going to call my pastor; I want him to come down and see what is going on."

Before that open-air meeting was over, about 500 people jammed onto the street. Standing right up front was the judge himself. Right alongside Judge Cotter was his liberal preacher, Peter Joshua. When Jack looked down and saw the judge, he decided to call on him for a word of testimony. Soon the judge was giving his testimony in the open-air meeting. Jack looked over and saw Peter Joshua and thought, "There's a good man for a word of testimony."

He went over and spoke to Peter Joshua and said, "Sir, would you give a word of testimony?"

Peter looked at Jack and said, "Here in the street? This doesn't seem like the greatest place to preach."

Jack dared this dignified formal Presbyterian minister to give his testimony right in the street. It was a real struggle for Peter Joshua. It was hard enough for him to share in the comfort of his own fashionable parish, but he couldn't find a way to say 'no' to Jack. Jack had a way of asking someone to do something, and when he asked, he expected it to be done. Jack never asked for his own good or for his own glory, but he asked to glorify and magnify the name of his wonderful Savior.

Soon this fashionable Presbyterian preacher was standing along with the judge on the rear of Jack Wyrtzen's car where "Old Glory" was flying. Peter Joshua did his best to preach a message on John 3:16. Not being used to street preaching, he almost lost his voice.

Later he wrote, "I wonder if Jack remembers smiling at me from his seat? What a radiant Christian. Like the measles... you can't get near him without catching his infectious joyfulness."

This pastor was so impressed with Jack and his team that he invited them to have a week of meetings in his church. He wanted Jack to be the evangelist. This was a bit of a problem because Jack was still working, and he only had two sermons.

Now, all of a sudden, Jack was responsible for an eight-day crusade. He preached the opening night and the closing night, and he led the singing every night. On the other nights, he invited speakers to come alongside and help him in the ministry. On the closing night, Jack gave the invitation, and many people found the Lord as their Savior.

At this time, Marge Smith was living at Peter Joshua's home and was now officially engaged to Jack. She told Jack she had observed the preacher smoking, going to shows, and doing many things that born-again believers should not do. So, Jack made sure when he spoke at Peter Joshua's church to speak on the subject of Christian separation.

When the week of meetings ended, Peter took his wife for a week's vacation. They spent their time reading their Bibles and praying and really got their lives straightened out. Subsequently, Peter became a great servant of Jesus Christ. No one had any idea that in a few years Jack would have the opportunity to baptize this pastor and his wife in the waters of Schroon Lake at the Word of Life Camp.

The meetings had gone so well that Jack definitely began to feel he should go into full-time evangelistic work. But, when would he make the break? Was this the moment? Was this God's time?

CHAPTER 5

The Family Room

...But as for me and my house, we will serve the LORD.
Joshua 24:15

They say behind every great man there is a great woman, and in Jack Wyrtzen's life this was no exception. Few women are cut out for a marriage to a man who is seldom home and consumed by work and obligations when he is home. But whenever Jack counted his blessings, which was every day, he always thanked the Lord for the unconditional love and support he got at home. Jack and Marge Wyrtzen enjoyed many years of happy and rewarding marriage and ministry together until Marge went to be with the Lord on New Year's Day, 1984.

The story of Jack and Marge Wyrtzen actually started many years before, on the day when Dr. and Mrs. Sidney Smith arrived at the home of the Gunns to adopt one of their children. Mrs. Gunn had died in a tragic fire, and the children were being cared for by an aunt. Grace, a curly haired tot of five, came running out through the door and right into the arms of the Smiths. The one they had come to adopt wasn't home, but Grace was, and she immediately won their hearts. So little Grace Gunn was taken, to be loved and cherished by the Smiths.

Her name had to be changed, since the Smiths already had a daughter named Grace. They named their new child Margaret, after Marge's mother, and, thus, she came to be known as Margaret Smith – known and loved by so many as simply "Marge."

Unfortunately, some people suffer with poor health their whole lives, and Marge was one of these people. Through the years she suffered from allergies and asthma, plus innumerable experiences of major and minor surgery. Her father, being a doctor and being aware of Marge's physical condition, had recommended that Marge not have any children. But God in a miraculous way gave her five wonderful children and many wonderful grandchildren.

Marge's frail health would cause her to develop a deep trust in the Lord as she often faced the anguish of hospitalization when Jack was out of town. He felt compelled to fulfill his calling to preach the Gospel, but he also longed to be with his wife. Jack would learn to commit his wife and family to the Lord until he could return to provide them with the tender care they frequently missed.

Marge was familiar with loneliness and pain, like many missionary wives, suffering mentally and physically while longing for her husband. She learned to cast all her care upon the Lord, knowing He would care for her.

On their wedding day, Marge had to wait for Jack to arrive. He broke a tooth and lost a filling that morning when he was playing baseball. His trip to the dentist caused him to be late for the wedding. As Marge waited for Jack to arrive, and while George Beverly Shea sang one number after another, the scent of the many beautiful floral arrangements began to get to her. The scent reminded her of the recent death of her mother, and Marge grew sick and feverish as she waited. Finally, he made it, and despite the illness and tears, Jack and Marge Wyrtzen were married on April 18, 1936.

Marge always had a wonderful personality, along with the tremendous gift of good humor. To hear her describe the details of the wedding and honeymoon would send anyone into fits of laughter. This, too, was fortunate, for God allowed much to happen in Marge's life. But out of these experiences of sickness and separation from the man she loved so deeply grew a life that knew the meaning of total dependence upon the Lord for everything. And this enabled her to counsel many a young person concerning the value of a life completely consecrated to the Lord. It wasn't always that way, of course, for when Jack and Marge first met, neither of them were saved. Jack and a friend were out for a walk one day, and they passed the Smith's home. Jack's friend knew Marge and her boyfriend, so they decided to drop in for a visit. It happened that Marge and her boyfriend were squabbling at the time, so it was easy for Jack to strike up an acquaintance.

It was spring, and, shortly after, Jack got another of his friends interested in hanging awnings as a means of earning some money. Wondering where to look for business, they thought of the Smiths, and set out to pay them a visit.

Although he usually hired professionals for the job, Dr. Smith agreed to let them take it on. As they were hanging awnings on the outside, there was Marge smiling at Jack from the inside. And so it was that they started dating, and Jack became her new boyfriend.

Throughout the history of Word of Life, Marge was a great encourager to Jack, and thousands of guests benefited from the warmth and graciousness her background and home life brought to the Word of Life Inn.

Marge also kept her eyes open to the personal needs of the Word of Life staff. She felt a personal responsibility toward each girl who came to work in the Word of Life office and also toward the wives of the Word of Life evangelists. She believed the Lord allowed her to be sick and lonely so she could encourage other girls to realize that God is able to meet every need known to the human heart.

She and Jack shared a very keen sensitivity to sin, and over the years she worked very hard with their children encouraging them to love the Lord and to put Him first and keep their lives devoted to Him. After all, their home was typical, their children normal, and their problems the same as any other family.

It is interesting to note that each of the children remembers the regularity and consistency of their family devotions, whether Dad was home or not. Their sick mother was consistent in leading her children to the Lord, and that was the most influential factor in their lives.

When their dad was home, morning devotions often took place at the breakfast table; many times Marge was too sick to be up in the morning. Evening devotions were at the dinner table and started out with "Egermeier's Bible Story Book" when the children were younger, then moved on to "Romans and I Corinthians for the Children's Hour" as they got older. Dave Wyrtzen commented that they must have gone through Romans and I Corinthians about 30 times, plus all the other Bible story books that were available. At bedtime, the children knelt beside their beds and prayed together with either Mother or Dad, or both.

All his children acknowledge that Jack led an absolutely consistent life at home. He was the same inside as outside, and this was a tremendous factor in their personal commitment to the Lord. Ron Wyrtzen says, "When I was younger, we read 'Egermeier's Bible Story Book,' and as I grew older, interest for the Bible increased because of these stories, and I gained a desire to read for myself." The children were regularly taught how much they should love the Lord and to pray to Him constantly. Dave Wyrtzen commented, "Dad taught me a real belief in the Word of God, a real emphasis on the importance of Scriptures in our lives and a real regard for his own personal values. I think he encouraged me in my own life to think through my opinions of different aspects of my life and especially my standards. Having a stringent attitude toward Christian separation and things like that, he might have been very forceful in that area. Yet, although we did have very strict rules, he did encourage us to really think it through for ourselves."

Betsy Oris, Jack's second daughter, reveals that the Wyrtzens were really just everyday people, facing a variety of situations and problems in their own family. She writes, "I remember that we had devotions frequently throughout the day, sometimes at breakfast, always after dinner and at bedtime. I think many times they were interesting because we got into very involved discussions. But there were other times when they were boring – partly because of my attitude toward things I wanted to do. If I hadn't planned to go out and play after supper, I didn't mind sitting there for devotions. Other times, anything we did would have been boring, because I wanted to get out and play. But I think that, on the whole, they were interesting and beneficial to us."

Ron says, "Dad, to me, was a man who really, really loved the Lord. While I was growing up, I found that everything he thought or anything that he preached to other people was lived in our home, and everything that we did was based on the Bible. I know a lot of times when we did things wrong, he would always take us into his study and show us out of the Word where we were wrong. Dad was a man who completely practiced what he preached, and he really loved the Lord. His whole desire, from what I can see, was for his family to live for the Lord and follow in His footsteps."

About his mother, Ron says, "We used to have a lot of fun. Mom used to talk to us and have devotions every night before we went to bed. I guess this is where you really learn to love your mother, especially if you're a boy, because with mom we always had lots of fun. She used to go out and do things with us. We would bake with her once in a while, or she would play games with us at night. She was always interested. She wasn't always busy with other things; her interest was always in her children."

When Jack was home, his time belonged to his family. "We would go to a baseball game or a football game. Usually once a year he would take us to West Point to watch the Army game there," Dave says. "Though he was away a lot, he was a good father to me. He took time with me; we played ball a lot, and we went to a lot of different places."

Betsy made a very good comment about her busy dad, and the way he filled her need as father when he was home. "He would not only do something with us, but he would do something that we wanted to do. It wasn't necessarily what he wanted to do, and I felt that he made excellent use of the time he spent with us, although it wasn't a lot. I always looked forward to when he came home. We went on picnics, went swimming, ice skating; we played ball together out in the yard – anything that we wanted to do."

Although he rarely told a joke, Jack loved life and enjoyed a hearty laugh. Serious himself – for life is no joke – he nevertheless surrounded himself with good-humored people.

This is one of the great joys of the Christian life. In fact, Jack believed that only born-again Christians know the real joy of living. He lived in a vital way for each day and its responsibilities. Tomorrow didn't worry him.

Part of the joie de vivre in the early days was an annual trip to Coney Island, where the family enjoyed the roller coaster, the whip, dodge-em cars, loop-the-loop, and all the rest. Jack's hilarious, contagious laugh could always be heard above the din and noise of the crowd.

The Barnum and Bailey Circus was another must – until the performers' clothing became too skimpy for Jack's liking. At that point, he made it quite clear to the management that until the show was cleaned up, neither he nor his family would be back to see that "cheap burlesque". Jack always was a man of conviction; he lived, ate, and slept to please the Lord. When the Bible speaks about the believer's body being the temple of the Holy Spirit, Jack believed it – and would do nothing to hurt or harm his body. If he discovered sin in a form of entertainment, he would cut it out of his and his family's life. Jack suffered no remorse whatever... only true joy in knowing he could please the Lord all the more.

One of his lasting pleasures was a love for horses. This probably dates back to his early years in the United States Cavalry Band. And, as long as he lived in New York or New Jersey, Jack never missed taking his family to see the rodeo when it came to Madison Square Garden.

Once the Lord led him into a camping ministry, Jack discovered that some of the wholesome family activities his family enjoyed became vital parts of the ministry. For example, at the Word of Life Ranch he started his own rodeo and rode in it weekly during the summer, heading up the parade, and taking part in some of the contests including a stick polo game on horseback.

A speedboat was a necessity to cross the water between the Word of Life Island and the mainland. Jack virtually flew across the lake from his home to the Island and loved every minute! He started the waterskiing program at Schroon Lake, and it became one of the most popular activities at camp.

Dogs were also a part of the Wyrtzen family's way of life. Two jet black Cocker Spaniels, Salt and Pepper, were well-beloved fixtures at Word of Life for more than ten years, and, in later years, a faithful Golden Retriever named Goldie could be seen almost daily at Word of Life Headquarters, waiting patiently outside Jack's office door.

When it came to fireplaces, Jack was like a child (he had four of them in his home). He wasn't satisfied with a little glowing flame and red embers; he wanted a roaring fire with huge blazing logs.

Jack also loved color. He was highly patriotic and flew the American flag over his home, all the camps, and the International Headquarters. The camps and main office building are also decorated with flags from all the countries where Word of Life is presently working, and these colorful insignias make a beautiful sight as they are unfurled on the sites of the Word of Life ministries.

Color was an essential part of Jack's wardrobe as well. Marge insisted that even if he was a grandfather, he shouldn't look like one if he hoped to relate to teenagers. Many adults were appalled, but most just laughed when they saw Jack walk into the dining room at the Word of Life Inn, dressed in a flowery shirt, a plaid sports jacket, and a boldly striped tie. At the same time, Jack's good taste was always evident, whether dressed colorfully for camp or more conservatively for other situations.

Neighborliness was another feature of the Wyrtzen family's lifestyle. They always took an interest in the families next door, down the street, or across the road. When the children were small, Marge held afternoon Bible classes for the children in the community. In this way, she got to know her children's school friends. At one time they even tried to adopt two of the youngsters they felt they could love and provide for as a family. Reaching families with the Good News of Jesus Christ was just as important to Jack as reaching the masses in rallies. Neighbors were often guests in the Wyrtzen home, where the love of Christ was demonstrated and shared on various occasions.

Today, all five Wyrtzen children are serving the Lord. Again, much of the credit goes to Marge, who with the Lord's help handled the bulk of their training because of Jack's absence.

Betsy said, "Mother did a good job in our disciplining, and she often had to do it alone because Daddy wasn't there. So, she had to make decisions on how to cope with a specific situation and with a particular child, because each of us had a different personality. I think I was one of the worst, because I was stubborn and would defy her. But I think she was wise in her discipline for many reasons. She didn't save up all the punishment for Dad to give, so she avoided making his homecoming something to fear because of the punishment he might give. Also, I can never remember her disciplining me in anger. She would send me to my room to think about it, and I always thought it was part of my punishment. But, of course, she told me later that her purpose was to allow her to get over her anger before she would punish me. And then after the discipline was over, we would pray about it, and she would make me see that it was not only that I had done wrong and hurt her or someone else, but also that I had hurt the Lord, and that was sinful. Once it was over, you weren't punished all day just because you had been bad in the morning. I don't remember my father's discipline too much; he wasn't home that often. When he was, I was usually on my best behavior. Overall, I think the discipline was very good and very consistent."

David doesn't remember being disciplined by his Dad; just by his Mother. He remembers at least two such occasions when he was small. At the same time, David says his Mother had a real love for them, and that many of the things he learned as a small child, he learned from her. "She spent a lot of time just talking to me when she was sick," he says, "and that meant a lot. Just like many of us, at certain times she could be really spiritual and come out with deep truths from the Word, and at other times she could be the opposite, because she was a real person."

Betsy claims, "Her most valuable attribute was her teaching us that being a mother was one of the best things in the world." She did things with us. She tried to be both parents to us. And she was quite a storyteller. I always enjoyed hearing about her life. I think she set a fine example as a Christian mother when we were growing up. I would say that I was led to the Lord through both my parents. I was always afraid of the dark, afraid that the Lord would come at night and take everyone else away and leave me alone in the dark. Of course, much of this had to do with whether I had been bad during the day. So, Mother would deal with me about this problem and give me assurance of my salvation and Dad also. It took a few times of 'getting saved' before I finally had the assurance that I was saved – when I was seven years old. After the specific decision was made with Dad in our living room, I never doubted again that I was a Christian.

"I think the greatest thing that Dad taught me was that he lived what he preached. If he told us to do something, he himself would do it also. There was no contradiction between what he said and what he did. The most important thing for both Mother and him was that they were consistent in living what they said."

David had an interesting comment about his Dad – describing him as a dominant leader, autocratic, forceful, set in his ways, willful, sometimes impulsive, and acting without thinking through. Yet, he speaks of his Dad as having a very real heart and that the Spirit of God was evident and at work through that combination of personal characteristics.

Ron reveals still other facets of Jack's personality and life. "Dad was a man who consistently and completely lived what he believed and preached. And because of his love for the Lord, the thing he was trying to get across to us more than anything else was why we, too, should give our whole heart to the Lord and live a life totally dedicated to Him. This has really helped me, because I have come to know that in life there is nothing else worth living for, except the Lord. And Dad encouraged me in this. I find the Christian life to be very exciting, very satisfying. I am not worried about my future. Whatever the Lord has for me, I know is best."

Another feature in the spiritual inheritance which Jack and Marge gave their children was the education they provided by sending them to a Christian high school in Florida. All five of the children were students there, and all profited tremendously from the experience. For example, Mary-Ann Wyrtzen Cox and her husband, Dave Cox, have incorporated many ideas from that school into the Word of Life Bible Institute which they founded in Sao Paulo, Brazil, in 1965. Although the Wyrtzens were often criticized for sending their children to boarding school, Jack and Marge constantly sought the assurance that God was leading all the way. They would never have made such "make or break" decisions about their children without that assurance. And time has proven that the Lord was indeed leading. All the Wyrtzen children have gone on to serve the Lord.

A further benefit has been the realization gained by all the children that the Christian home is highly important. Mary-Ann, the oldest, is a mother of four, and, along with her husband, Dave, followed the same ideals set before her by her parents. She and Dave talked, prayed, taught, and disciplined their children in the home they established in Brazil, just as Jack and Marge did with their youngsters in years gone by.

To each of the children the family is a very close group, something ordained by God. Brothers, sisters, and in-laws alike have always been a closely-knit unit. Jack and Marge spent many hours writing letters, phoning, counseling, guiding, and encouraging the family – for this was ever a home where the Lord was preeminent.

That Jack had a larger "family" was abundantly evident after his wife, Marge, went Home to be with the Lord on New Year's Day, 1984. Thousands of comforting and encouraging letters, books, tracts and booklets poured in from people around the world who had been touched by the Wyrtzen's ministry over the years.

One dear friend, Dr. Wendell Kempton, sent Jack a booklet concerning what happens between death and the Rapture, written in 1880 by a great soul-winning YMCA leader when that organization was still a stronghold of true Christian testimony. Republished by Word of Life under the title,

"In The Meantime," this booklet has ministered to tens of thousands of aching hearts needing comfort from the Scripture. In an epilogue to that publication, Jack tells in his own words about that day Marge Wyrtzen was called to Heaven:

"When my wife, Marge, went Home to be with the Lord, she was happy and joyous all day long. That morning she made out a check for God's work never realizing this was the last check she would ever write. We went to church in the morning at Word of Life Inn and then at night we attended our own church here in Schroon Lake. Afterwards, we were headed for a friend's house when my wife said, 'Honey, I can't breathe!' She went Home to be with the Lord in my arms. 'She was not for God took her' (Genesis 5:24). It was like the Rapture. Soul and spirit were immediately with the Lord. For her, 'death was gain' (Philippians 1:21). 'Absent from the body. Present with the Lord' (2 Corinthians 5:8). The doctor who examined her later on that evening said, 'I never know what to say to a man when his wife has died. All I can say is she's dead.' A few moments later a nurse came over and said, 'If I were religious, I would pray with you, but I'm not.' Thank God, we who love the Savior have a hope beyond the grave. My wife being dead yet speaketh, for she was a great witness and soul-winner ever since she met the Savior at age 19. Now Home with the Lord, her testimony continues to carry on, through our children and the many who came to know the Lord through her witness."

Jack said he was touched by the outpouring of love, comfort and encouragement that came to him in the time after Marge's death. But despite the heartfelt concern of hundreds of friends, the sense of loss was great. Jack himself did not want loneliness to sidetrack his obedience to the command, that ye present your bodies a living sacrifice, holy, acceptable unto God, which is your reasonable service. (Romans 12:1). So, Jack prayed earnestly for the Lord to lead him in this difficult trial, either to give him strength to carry on alone if that was His will or to bring a special helpmate into his life.

While he had preached to and counseled thousands on every conceivable aspect of Christian life, Jack was never too proud to honor the counsel and advice of other godly men. One day Dr. John MacArthur, President of The Master's College and a great author and Bible teacher, had come to speak at Word of Life Inn. During a break between meetings, the two began talking together about Jack's situation, and Dr. MacArthur said, "Jack, you don't have the luxury of teenagers to date around a lot. When you meet her, both of you will fully agree it is God's will. Find a woman who has had a good first marriage, and since you had a good first marriage, it should be a good match." Jack took this advice to heart and began to study 1 Timothy 5, about the twelve qualifications widows must meet to be supported by the church. "If I'm going to support a widow," Jack thought to himself, "I'd better look for a gal who meets those qualifications, too."

People who knew Jack Wyrtzen knew he was a man of action – but this was because the Lord hurried him, and not because he was trying to hurry the Lord. Through prayer and Bible study, Jack felt God was leading him to remarry, but, in his heart, Jack was content to let God work out the details in His own perfect timing. *It is not in man who walks to direct his own steps* (Jeremiah 10:23b). Those who try to direct their own steps will go wrong. *The steps of a good man are ordered by the LORD* (Psalm 37:23). As he read through Psalm 37 and came to verse 4, Jack felt a great peace and thrill as he read, Delight yourself also in the LORD, And He shall give you the desires of your heart. The Lord would give Jack his heart's desire! He had no need to worry, but only to delight in the Lord!

And whatever you ask in My name, that I will do, that the Father may be glorified in the Son. If you ask anything in My name, I will do it... Ask, and you will receive, that your joy may be full. (John 14:13-14, 16:24). Jack asked the Lord for a "helper fit for him" (Genesis 2:18), and God answered in an unexpected way.

Over the years, Jack attended countless Bible meetings and conferences, but always as the speaker. He never remembered attending a conference where he was not speaking – except one. In early 1986 he had just returned from Israel, completing a hectic travel schedule, when his dear friend, Dr. Wendell Kempton of the Association of Baptists for

World Evangelism, invited Jack to be his personal guest at the group's upcoming conference in Bermuda. "Maybe a little break wouldn't be a bad idea," Jack thought. So, he went.

The second day of the conference was marked by a motorbike accident which left one attendee, Ruth Mensch, in the hospital with serious injuries. Throughout the week Jack kept hearing about the injured woman's companion, Joan Steiner. Joan was spending every day of her Bermuda Bible conference vacation visiting her injured friend at the hospital. Jack could see right away that this was a remarkable woman who had great compassion. But when Dr. Kempton and other friends offered to introduce her to him or invite her to dinner, Jack was not interested. "After all," laughed Jack, "I've been meeting a lot of widows the past couple of years!" Still, because Jack had been the one to first introduce the widowed Dr. Kempton to his second wife, Ruth, Dr. Kempton felt entitled to return the favor and kept talking about this "Joan Steiner" throughout the week.

The conference was coming to an end, and the delegates were invited to attend a day cruise. Jack wouldn't have missed it, and Joan signed up because she had had no recreation all week. As Jack boarded the shuttle bus from the hotel, there was only one empty seat. Across the aisle were missionary friends from Hong Kong, and Jack turned to them for a chat. After a long conversation with the missionaries, it dawned

on Jack that he was being impolite to the person seated next to him. He turned around, explained about his missionary friends, and then said, "I'm Jack Wyrtzen. What's your name?"

"Joan Steiner."

"Joan Steiner!" This was the woman Dr. Kempton had been telling Jack about all week, the one Jack wasn't interested in meeting! Jack burst out laughing with one of his trademark guffaws; Joan was absolutely astonished.

"Why are you laughing?" Joan asked.

"Don't worry. I'll tell you about it later," Jack replied.

Once aboard ship, Joan told several friends that her companion, Ruth, would be able to travel home with her the next day. The cruise coordinator asked Jack to make this happy announcement to the passengers and to pray for Ruth's continued recovery.

"Well, well," thought Jack to himself delightedly. "Maybe the Lord does answer prayer in unusual ways!"

"I really don't know much about your girlfriend," Jack said, turning to Joan. "Would you come to the captain's quarters as my guest and give an update, and then I'll pray?"

Joan agreed. But Bermuda is a warm country, and after sitting together at length in the captain's quarters, it became uncomfortably hot. "Why don't we go out to the bow for some air," Jack suggested. And before they knew it, it was 1 a.m.; they were back in the hotel coffee shop still talking together over ice cream. Jack had planned to meet missionary friends from Brazil at the beach the next morning at 7:30 to sing and pray. Would Joan like to go? She would – and as the two joined hands at the beach the next morning for group devotions and prayer, Jack admitted to saying one of his longer prayers!

Of course, when the conference ended, Jack felt a responsibility to call Joan, to make sure she arrived home safely, and inquire about her injured friend. So, he telephoned her home in Leavenworth, Kansas, the day after the conference, and every night that following week. The next week Jack "happened" to be traveling through Kansas City on his way to a meeting overseas. Could he stop and visit? And when he got back from England, could she meet him at the New York City airport and drive up to see the Adirondack Mountains?

"Joan is the type of woman who would usually say no," admits Jack. "So, at first she wondered if she was crazy to accept my invitations." But as John MacArthur had told Jack so many months earlier, "When the Lord brings the two of you together, both of you will fully agree it is His will."

During the visit to the Adirondacks, Jack and Joan were engaged. Then on May 9, 1986, the two were wed in Lansing, Kansas, in a ceremony performed by Dave Wyrtzen and Joan's church pastor, Bill Stone.

Why was Joan at the Bermuda conference? Her first husband had died of cancer, and her three children were grown and living on their own. Though she was an accomplished business executive, Joan went to Bermuda seeking God's will for her life – and in His perfect timing, she found it!

In a letter to Jack shortly before their marriage, Joan wrote, "I do have a few things that are mine alone to give you, some promises I hope soon to be able to fulfill, and you can hold me to them because I view them only as a labor of my love toward you. I will pray for you daily. I will respect you at all times. I will be submissive to you. I will love you completely. I will always be honest to you so you can trust me completely and confidently. I will strive to be an asset to your life and a complement to you in every way. I will never do anything knowingly to hinder you. I will see to your every need. I will make a home for you that is a place of rest, a home you will be proud of. I will always strive to show the fruit of the Spirit in my life, so that you will never need to be ashamed of me. I thank God every day for bringing you into my life, for He has filled me with so much love and joy and wonder over it all!"

To look at Joan is to see the fruit of the Spirit. One of the first things Jack noticed about her was the love, joy, and big smile she always showed toward others. Joan traveled across America and the world with Jack, providing the companionship and support he needed to maintain the busy speaking schedule necessary for the head of such a large, international evangelistic organization as Word of Life, through which untold thousands have heard the glorious Gospel of Christ.

Looking back over more than a half century of serving the Lord, Jack enjoyed the great reward and satisfaction of seeing the fruitful ministry God allowed him to enjoy. But, he counted it an even greater joy to see his outreach continue in the lives of his family.

CHAPTER 6

The Wiring

...my God shall supply all your need...
Philippians 4:19

"You're going to live by what?" "Faith."

"What do you mean 'faith'?"

"By that I mean we're going to trust God to supply our needs. I'm quitting my job. From now on we'll just have to trust the Lord for everything." This was what Jack said to his relatives on that all-important day when he took the big step.

"How can you do it at a time like this? You're a married man! You have many responsibilities; what about your baby? How can you leave your good job behind?"

Yes, they were asking good questions. Jack knew it sounded stupid, but once again he was stepping out by faith. He had asked the Lord to give them so many meetings for the month of November that he wouldn't be able to take care of his job responsibilities. The Lord answered his prayer and gave him 45 speaking engagements during the one month of November.

In 1940 Jack had begun a Tuesday morning broadcast over a station in Brooklyn, WBBC. It wasn't much of a station, but it was an opportunity, and the time was free. Mail was coming in and people were enthused with the program. The radio program, on top of his many meetings, had caused Jack to make the decision to step out by faith. Now what was he to do? He could go full time with Word of Life and possibly scrape together about $30 a week for his family, but even that would be by faith. Or else he could get involved in another Christian organization. They offered him a starting salary of $60-65 a week. It was a big decision. Both were opportunities in full-time service – one with a lot of money and the other with little money.

Jack and Marge did what they had now become accustomed to do every time they faced problems. They prayed about it and the more they prayed, the more they felt that they should stick with their own group, Word of Life. They had real peace concerning their decision.

The next day was Tuesday, time for their weekly broadcast on station WBBC in Brooklyn, New York. They arrived confident in the Lord's leading in their lives and determined under God to follow through with the decision they had made. They would make the big announcement on the radio. When they arrived that morning in Brooklyn, they found the station closed; a sign on the door said, "Out of Business." Now where to go? What to do next? Jack was now living by faith. He had been counting on the radio program... now it was out of business.

He immediately began to think of some other radio station that could possibly carry the Word of Life program, perhaps on a more powerful station. He heard about WHN. Jack was interested, but the manager wasn't – he didn't want any religion on his station.

Besides being a tireless worker, Jack had inherited a tremendously strong will. He just didn't give up easily. Jack knew what he wanted and knew how to get it. For the moment, the door was closed, but it would open. It was hard to know God's will, but Jack knew God could and would open some door.

Over at WHN, a young salesman named Marty Glickman saw Jack's very aggressive request. Unaware of the previous negative decision and anxious for some new business, Marty drew up a 13-week contract, handed it to Jack and told him to sign on the dotted line. Now the only problem was the $1,750 that would be due before the first broadcast. Not only were they now living by faith, but here was another tremendous step by faith. They had prayed for the open door, and here was the opportunity. Jack and the team decided to trust God for the impossible. Their prayers were answered, and before the first program went on the air, $1,760 had come in – a surplus of $10 – this was all Jack needed. Now he was sure of the step of faith he had taken to move out on the promise that God would supply all their needs. Since they were going to have a radio broadcast on Saturday night, why not get an auditorium? Why not have a radio rally? Would anyone come on a Saturday night for a religious meeting? Jack looked around; where would be the best place? Where do people go on Saturday in the New York area? Only one place... Times Square. Jack checked around and soon found the old Alliance Gospel Tabernacle on 44th Street and 8th Avenue in Manhattan. It looked like just the place. Not only was it in Times Square, the sin capital of the city, but the old Alliance Gospel Tabernacle was the place where a missionary pastor, Dr. A.B. Simpson, Founder of the Christian and Missionary Alliance, had preached the Gospel for so many years.

At exactly 7:30 p.m., October 25, 1941, Word of Life hit the airwaves for the first time... "Word of Life Fellowship presents Jack Wyrtzen with words of life for the youth around the world." This exciting program has been heard ever since, opening with the well-known verse that Word of Life uses as its motto, Holding forth the word of life; that I may rejoice in the day of Christ, that I have not run in vain, neither labored in vain. (Philippians 2:16)

This worldwide program opened with the music theme, "Wonderful Words of Life," then presented a variety of special music, dynamic testimonies from people in all walks of life, and concluded with a straightforward Bible message from Jack Wyrtzen. Thousands have responded to the direct, uncompromising appeal.

The station, WHN, which had already signed a contract with Word of Life for 13 weeks, increased its transmission wattage from 5,000 to

50,000 during the first month of broadcasting, giving the program an even greater potential audience. The first radio rally was a great success, but the following week the attendance was down from 250 to 150. Many people would have been discouraged at this point, but not Jack. He was sure, absolutely certain, that God had directed him, and by faith he was claiming the promises of God. By the third Saturday in January, the auditorium was packed out, and many found the Lord as their Savior. For many succeeding years, that was the story of the radio rallies.

Jack was able to gather around him a group of men who were vitally interested in his ministry. Some of the early speakers were Erling C. Olsen, Horace Dean, Ralph Davis, James Bennett, Ted Fix and Forrest Forbes. Some were musicians: Norman Clayton, the author of many wonderful hymns and choruses, and Carlton Booth, a famous tenor soloist.

The rallies began increasing in size every week, and the number of stations carrying the program grew rapidly. The Gospel Tabernacle was now too small. The next place was the Mecca Temple that could seat about 3,000. That was the site of the first victory rally in May 1942 which would proclaim the Gospel and ask God to grant our soldiers victory on the battlefields of Europe and the Pacific. Many people hoped for a good meeting, but Jack was sure God was going to pack the place. He had caught a vision for this rally as he lay awake the previous night. More than 3,000 people jammed into the auditorium. The speaker that night was Walter McDonald, better known as Happy Mac. Many souls were saved.

From there they moved to the historic Carnegie Hall in New York City. Just to rent the auditorium cost $700. Again, they took this step by faith. Jack found out they were advertising, "The best tunes of all come from Carnegie Hall." He said, "Let's go over and prove that they are right."

They announced on the radio they were going to Carnegie Hall for a rally. That night there were 3,000 inside and 3,000 outside. Wanting to see for himself, he struggled through the crowd to get past the lobby and out into the street. Just then, a big Irish policeman grabbed Jack and said, "Hey, are you the guy responsible for bringing all these people to

New York City and for blocking up all this traffic?" He looked at Jack and said, "Listen, if you're going to do this again, why don't you rent Madison Square Garden where you can handle a crowd like this?" Jack thought this was really funny, so at the meeting that night he stood up and told the people about the Irish policeman and what he had said. Everybody laughed with him... what a joke!

The following week Jack was in a meeting in upstate New York in a little Baptist church. It was a rainy Friday night, and Jack was giving a report on the rally at Carnegie Hall, including the incident with the policeman. Everybody started to laugh, except one man who shouted out, "Amen!" It seemed to ring a bell with him. At the end of the meeting, he came up and gave his card to Jack and said, "I'm going to pray about this for two weeks, and at the end of the two weeks I'm going to tell you what to do." Jack and the team also began to pray.

Two weeks later this man, George Traber, sent a letter that said, "I prayed about it and feel the Lord wants you to have a rally in Madison Square Garden. I'm enclosing a check for $1,000." Now Jack was really on the spot. A $1,000 check was great, but where would he ever get $6,000 more just to pay the rent for one night in the Garden, to say nothing of the advertising and all the other expenses that would be involved.

Jack again began to pray, and the Lord revealed to him something that had seldom been done before or since. In some very visible or audible way the Lord gave Jack the assurance there would not only be 20,000 people inside, but there would be 10,000 out in the street. Jack was so sure of this that when he had his meetings night after night, he told people there would be 20,000 people inside and 10,000 outside, and if they were going to get in at all, they had better get there early.

Many of the prominent preachers in New York City didn't believe him. They said the day of mass evangelism had ended with Billy Sunday; that the whole idea was ridiculous and stupid. They warned the people not to go. But Jack kept praying, and he kept on preaching. Jack called up his friend, Carlton Booth. "Carl, what do you think?"

"Maybe we'd better retrace our steps," Carl said.

The time was coming close for the rally; it was planned for April 1, 1944. It was wartime, and Jack had lined up all kinds of colonels, captains, and commanders who were born again to give their testimonies. The closing message would then be given by Jack himself.

Two days before the rally, Jack received word from the War Department that no man in the military would be allowed to appear at the rally. It seemed that every time Jack took a step of faith, the devil was there to close the door or put obstacles in the way.

Right from the very beginning when Jack had made his decision to go full time with Word of Life, the devil had been busy. But Jack came back fighting; he wasn't going to let the enemy get the victory this time or any time. He later commented, "Actually, it scared the life out of me. All we knew how to do was to pray." So down on their knees they went once again.

They got in touch with some friends... Phil Benson, president of the Dime Savings Bank, Bob Nelson, an executive of a large corporation, and Erling Olsen, who knew an admiral in Washington. While all these men were busy working, Jack and the team were praying.

Then things got more complicated. Right before the rally, Don, Jack's only son at the time, suddenly became very sick. At this time, Marge was expecting their third child. To anybody else it would have been overwhelming, but Jack knew God had a plan. He knew that all things work together for good to those who love the Lord. The day before the rally, Betsy Wyrtzen was born, Don's fever broke, and nobody knows exactly what happened behind the scenes, but just before the rally, a telephone call came stating all military personnel would be allowed to appear.

The rally was to start at 7:30 p.m., with the doors opening at 6:30 p.m., but so many people arrived in the afternoon that by 4:30 p.m. there were thousands of people in the street, and the doors had to be opened early. Instead of 7:30 p.m. the rally started at 6:30 p.m., and according to police estimates, it happened just as God had told Jack. There were 20,000 inside and more than 10,000 out in the street.

Amplifiers were rigged outside so everyone could hear, and many were saved even as they walked up and down the streets. God again proved His faithfulness as hundreds found the Lord Jesus Christ as their Savior.

CHAPTER 7

The Attic

...Lord, what do you want me to do?
Acts 9:6

One night Jack was preaching, "Only one life, 'twill soon be past; only what's done for Christ will last." Later, as he drove home, he kept going over in his mind... was he really doing what the Lord wanted him to do? Surely, he was living by faith; he had left his job. The radio program was going great, the rallies were drawing big crowds, and hundreds of people were claiming the Lord as their Savior, but was this it? Or should he lift up his eyes to foreign lands as well?

Jack knew that God's will for his life was to preach the Gospel, but now, geographically, where was the place the Lord wanted him most? Was it here in America or was it in some foreign land? This was a constant struggle in Jack's life until he went to a meeting and heard Ralph Davis, veteran missionary and general secretary of the Africa Inland Mission. He spoke of the tremendous needs of that great continent and of the open doors and opportunities to proclaim the Gospel. After listening to Ralph Davis, Jack turned to Marge and said, "Marge, I believe the Lord would have us go as missionaries to Africa. This is where the Lord would have us go – Africa."

Everything was great until, sometime later, he met Bob Williams. Bob was a pioneer missionary to Borneo, and as he told of the Dayak people in that great needy land, Jack's heart seemed to come alive. Was this the place the Lord would have him go?

So, after listening to Bob Williams, Jack was sure God was calling him to Borneo. He was all keyed up about Borneo until he later heard another missionary tell of another tremendous field and its great opportunity. Jack was really bewildered. He was being brought face to face with a second great crisis in his life. The first had been whether he should live by faith; the second was the mission field. Should he go or stay?

The challenge of Paul Fleming of New Tribes Mission was the most disturbing, and it all hinged on the last command of Jesus Christ. He constantly emphasized the truth that every man, woman, and child in the world had a greater right to hear the Gospel once than our right to hear it twice. Being deeply moved by this message, Jack was determined under God that he would go to some unevangelized country. He and Marge were more willing to go than to stay in New York.

Of course, they could not ignore the fact there were also millions of unsaved young people in the United States, and God was giving them a harvest of souls in meetings and rallies. Jack didn't want to be influenced by his own preferences, so there was a fierce struggle within his heart.

One night he said to Marge, "I can't take it any longer. I'm going up to the attic; I'm going to wait on the Lord until he shows me without a doubt what His will is for me." Jack could go on no longer without absolute certainty of what he was doing. There in the attic on his knees before an open Bible, he began to read in Proverbs 3:5-6: *Trust in the Lord with all thine heart; and lean not unto thine own understanding. Trust in the Lord! Trust in the Lord! In all thy ways acknowledge Him, and He shall direct thy paths.*

The hours of heart-searching brought him out of the dark into the green pastures of God's peace. That experience in the early hours of that morning marked one of the turning points in the ministry of Word of Life. Jack was confident God wanted him to stay, but now he had a missionary vision.

Little did Jack realize that day in the attic that even though the Lord wanted him to stay home in America, He would allow him to travel to many countries and preach the Gospel to millions of people. Jack knew God's will for him was to stay in America, yet the Lord gave him the desire to preach to multitudes elsewhere.

Jack's first missionary journey was to Mexico in 1945 with two companions. Jack tells it like this: "We left at 5:00 in the morning for Mexico City and arrived at our destination in the early evening by car. I'll never forget the thrill of the first night as we walked into an Indian village with a guide and a little donkey carrying our luggage. There on this high tableland of the Mazahuas, nine thousand feet above sea level, among lowly Indian huts, we were greeted by the young lady who had spent eight years translating portions of the Bible and songs into the tribal language. While we were eating dinner, the Indians started arriving for the meeting. Her front room was small, and it seemed full when 25 Indians had come in. We asked them if they wanted to sing. Which one of the 104 hymns would they like to learn? They wanted to know all of them! Beginning with number one, we sang for a while and then more Indians arrived. Then there were 70 in the room. This would go on each evening from dinner until 11 or 12 o'clock. The Indians smiled when we tried to sing in their language. One after another got up with radiant faces and told how the Lord had wonderfully saved them."

"I learned later that, about 10 years before, a Mexican believer had come to this tribe with prayer and friendliness, winning many to Christ. The price this faithful missionary paid for his testimony would put us to shame. They told us he had been beaten and left for dead once after his teeth had been knocked out and his head crushed in. What suffering for preaching the Gospel to a people in a land where evil religious systems had opposed the light of God's Word for four hundred years! This man came back again to minister, and his enemies were put to flight. The blood of martyrs is still the seed of the church. In the years following, it was reported there were approximately five hundred believers among the Mazahuas."

"The next morning after we arrived, we were up early visiting the homes of the Indian Christians. The pigs, the sheep, and the Indians all lived in the same houses, but this didn't seem to bother anyone at all. Finally, it came time for us to leave, and we felt like Paul when he left the Ephesian church. The local elders accompanied us on an hour walk to the railroad station. The train was an hour late, so we had a little service. After we attempted to minister the Word a while, we asked them to do likewise. I'll never forget an Indian named Leonardo, who stood to his feet and read from Luke 1:1-4. Finally, he looked at us and said, 'There are 77,000 people in my tribe, and they are scattered all through these mountains in little villages.' Then with grim determination he said, 'Brethren, even if it costs me my life, I'm going to carry the Gospel to them, for they have never heard.' It was hard to say good-bye. When the train came, we waved until we could not see them anymore."

What a joy to know, "When the roll is called up yonder, we'll be filled with joy and wonder when we see the blood-bought number. Some from every tribe and nation will be there!"

In May 1946, another missionary journey materialized when Jack and Marge, Carlton and Ruth Booth, and Harry Bollback toured the British Isles. The blessing of the Lord was evident as thousands attended the rallies and hundreds professed faith in Christ. Each Saturday night the broadcast originated from various cities of the United Kingdom: London, Cardiff, Glasgow, and Belfast.

Then another tremendous door of opportunity opened up – the teaching and preaching of God's Word at the United States Military Academy at West Point. Willing workers had obtained the privilege of distributing New Testaments to the officers and cadets. The Academy chaplain had approved only a five-minute service of dedication, and he planned to take the rest of the service. However, word got around quickly that Jack was going to speak at West Point, and many thought he was speaking for the entire service, so friends began to call the chaplain, much to his annoyance. No one knows how the report became so exaggerated. The chaplain thought he should at least become acquainted with Jack, since so many people were calling, and from that meeting a warm, personal friendship developed between Jack and the chaplain.

When the day of the formal presentation service came, the chaplain decided to give the entire time to the young evangelist. This opened the door for Jack to keep a Bible study class going at the Academy for many years. It was at this time he reached many military men for the Lord Jesus Christ. Little did he realize how God was putting the picture together. In a very short time, he would need help from some of these military men as he traveled around the world.

During the Korean War, Jack arrived in Japan expecting to minister to our fighting men in Korea. Actually, he took the whole trip by faith, for his Korean visa had not come through. Miraculously, God opened the door and enabled Jack, accompanied by Glenn Wagner, Don Robertson and Vic Springer, to minister to a quarter of a million men on the front lines in Korea. For a few days it appeared utterly impossible to reach fighting men; all seemed hopeless until General Harrison arranged for Jack to have an interview with General Harkins.

Staff members held a prayer meeting and claimed the promise in Ephesians 3:20, Now unto Him that is able to do exceedingly abundantly above all that we ask or think, according to the power that worketh in us. They broke the text down by asking, "What do we want? Permission. Besides that, we need food, equipment, trucks, and gas." This, to them, was "exceedingly abundantly above."

Inside, as the interview was going along, General Harkins remembered Jack Wyrtzen from his Bible class days at West Point. It happened that he was a personal friend of General Maxwell Taylor, and within 30 minutes, permission was granted from General Taylor for everything they needed. This was government orders! Literally everything was at their disposal to get the job done. Triumphantly, Jack told Robbie and the rest of the team, and they all shouted, "Hallelujah!"

The meetings with the troops were ordained of God. With a Gospel of John in one hand and a gun in the other, the men listened to the message. Their helmets were the only chairs available. Yes, God had given to Jack what he had asked for.

In 1972 Jack had the opportunity of returning to Korea for a special 15-day crusade. Since his first visit in 1952, great changes had taken place economically, politically, and especially spiritually. Jack spoke at the military academies of the Korean Air Force and Army. Since most of the meetings were with military personnel, the Korean Air Force provided a helicopter to transport Jack and the team from base to base. In one tremendous meeting, more than 14,000 soldiers were marched onto the drill field, and for two hours Jack had the opportunity to tell them what God had done in his life when he was in the army. He then gave the invitation for those who wanted to receive the Lord Jesus Christ as Savior.

God gave to Jack something very unique in giving an invitation. He had no set pattern as far as the mechanics were concerned. Sometimes he would ask his audience to raise their hands if they have received the Lord into their hearts; other times it was the request, "Stand up and come forward." The method is unimportant. The results are what really count. They always came and in great numbers, and the majority of them were really sincere decisions. In Korea it was no exception. Jack gave the invitation to these 14,000 soldiers, and more than 8,000 immediately stood to their feet. The response was so great and spontaneous that the chaplain couldn't believe what he had seen with his own eyes. He personally went over Jack's message and asked the soldiers the second time to make decisions. The response was even greater.

God had allowed Jack to stay in America to preach the Gospel to multitudes of young people, and now he was traveling around the world as a missionary. But, still, he didn't stop.

Jack looked and saw multitudes in India, a land of 340 million gods.

What an opportunity to tell people of the only true and living God – the Lord Jesus Christ! There was South America where God blessed in a significant way during a crusade in the city of Sao Paulo. In an auditorium that could hardly seat 4,000, crowds were so great that finally, on the closing day, three consecutive rallies had to be held. There was Africa, the land Jack had always dreamed about, the land of his first missionary vision. More than 500,000 people came to the meetings, with approximately 7,000 signing cards to indicate their decision to receive Jesus Christ as their Savior.

Everyone thought it would be an impossibility to get behind the Iron Curtain, into Russia and Poland, and yet God, in a miraculous way, opened the door for Jack to hold an evangelistic crusade for a week in Warsaw, Poland. Night after night the church was filled as great crowds came. Jack had total freedom and liberty to preach the Gospel, and many found the Lord as their Savior.

In 1947 a young man in New Zealand tuned in to the Word of Life broadcast on station HCJB from Quito, Ecuador. He heard Jack tell of the camp he was starting in the United States of America. As Ces Hilton listened in his home, he said, "Lord, if Jack Wyrtzen can do it in America, then we can do it here in New Zealand as well." By faith he started. He received weekly instructions and encouragement through the Word of Life broadcast, as well as personal correspondence with Jack. For years Jack was invited to speak at a camp called Kiwi Ranch that was started in New Zealand, which can accommodate 300 young people each week.

Jack's orders from the Lord were to go into all the world and preach the Gospel to every creature. He settled that a long time ago on his knees

up in the attic before the open Book, when he read: Trust in the Lord with all your heart; and lean not unto thine own understanding; in all thy ways acknowledge Him, and He shall direct thy paths.

CHAPTER 8

The Landscaping

And whatever things you ask in prayer, believing, you will receive. Matthew 21:22

Jack Wyrtzen had just returned to his office after his trip to the British Isles in 1947 when the telephone rang.

"Hello, Jack," said his secretary. "There is a real estate agent here who wants to speak to you personally. May I send her in?"

While the agent was being ushered in, Jack tried to imagine what this person could possibly want to talk about.

"Jack," the realtor said, "I know you work with young people. I heard your program on the radio and feel that you ought to open a camp for young people. I have a beautiful piece of property up in the Adirondack Mountains on Schroon Lake."

Jack politely informed the real estate agent that they were not at all interested in starting a youth camp, but she kept talking. Jack continued to insist he was not interested in a youth camp. She finally showed him some photographs of a beautiful island in the middle of Schroon Lake which was for sale.

With this the agent said, "Look, Mr. Wyrtzen, suppose I leave the pictures here with you, and if you are interested, get in touch with me." She left. Jack began to look over the pictures. It looked tremendous and seemed like a great opportunity. As Jack sat at his desk, he remembered that not so long ago at another lake he had talked to his friend, Al Kunz, director of a youth camp in Speculator, New York, about the possibility of a Word of Life camp.

Al had invited Jack to be one of his speakers. One day when Jack was standing on the shores of that beautiful lake looking across to the mountains, he turned to Mr. Kunz and said, "I'm certainly glad God never called me to start a camp for young people."

Even as he sat in his office that day in June reviewing those beautiful pictures of the island, he bowed his head, "Lord, is this the next step? Is this what you have for us now?" Already the work was growing. The budget had already tripled since Jack had stepped out by faith. The radio program, rallies, plus some 65 missionaries who they were supporting all around the world, were really straining the budget. Could they take another step of faith? Could they really trust God for more? As Jack looked at the pictures, he thought, "Well, it won't cost us anything to drive up and look at the place."

Within hours Jack, Marge, and Fred Scharmann, along with some other friends, drove up to Schroon Lake. They were impressed with the beauty of the mountains as they drove along. Soon they were standing on the shores of crystal clear Schroon Lake, looking across to the island.

Jack was thinking, "Lord, will this someday be Word of Life Island?" Already, Jack was praying. Soon the group was on its way across the lake. Fred Scharmann was seated in the back of the rowboat; one of the younger members of the team was in the middle rowing, and, as usual, Jack was up front giving the orders: "A little bit more to the right, a little bit to the left," as he picked the place where the boat was to land.

It was a tremendous island, but it really didn't look like the pictures. Oh, the big trees were there, and Schroon Lake was there, but the buildings were in a terrible state, and the lawns were all overgrown with weeds and bushes. As the party headed back toward the beach, they got down on their knees before getting into the boat, and Jack prayed. As they got up, they were sure this was to be Word of Life Island.

A new direction was now in sight for Word of Life. God had enlarged Jack's vision. This would be the next step. Jack contacted the real estate agency and was informed the owner was asking $125,000 for it. To this he replied, "If we're ever to have the island, then God must give it to us on a miracle basis." Any price would have been too much. As usual, there was no money available. Word of Life has never had a financial reserve; Jack felt he would be embarrassed to meet the Lord if he had money in the bank instead of having it invested in the lives of people. Jack called the real estate agent and told her he would like to meet with the owner, as he was interested in making a bona fide offer to purchase the island. He told the agent, "Word of Life, after much prayer, has decided to make an offer of $25,000 for the island." The agent, however, refused to present the offer. "This is much too low," she said. "The owner would never consider it."

But as God would have it, soon afterward, Jack was speaking at a local church and learned the owner's name through someone's offhand remark. Therefore, Jack was able to present the $25,000 offer directly to Miss Clark, the owner, who was one of the surviving relatives of O.N.T. Clark, the spool and thread company. She was informed this Christian venture would benefit countless thousands of teenagers around the world, and upon hearing this, Miss Clark accepted the $25,000 offer.

Jack gave the real estate agent a check for $1,000 to make a legal binder. Even the $1,000 had to be borrowed, since Word of Life had no money to even get started in such a tremendous investment. The next question was, "Where would the $25,000 come from?" And they needed it in thirty days! God, in a miraculous way, moved upon the hearts of the people – 47 in all – who gave generously to meet the need of purchasing the island. The first year was one of work, work, work, as volunteer groups literally transformed the island. Windows were put back into houses; the lawns were cut, and the buildings painted.

Some Council members came and looked over the island and thought that Jack had made a mistake this time. This didn't look like a very good investment. There was a lot to repair; and time was running out; soon camp would be opening. But Jack, a man of tremendous vision and great drive who really knew what God wanted him to do, left nothing unturned in getting the job done. Jack pitched in himself to do much of the work, along with Marge, who did all the cooking for the entire staff during those months of hard work. Many times, when Marge stood over the gas stove there in the kitchen, she remembered her days at Pinebrook where God had taught her so many wonderful lessons. And now the Lord was allowing Jack and Marge to prepare another camp to reach countless young people with the Word of God.

From that simple beginning in 1947, God has blessed in a remarkable way. The present facilities are a tribute to the glory of God. Every year there have been tremendous improvements, and a week on the Island has been the means of changing the lives of literally thousands of people. In the ministry of Word of Life and in the life of Jack, every time there was tremendous blessing, the devil seemed to attack harder than ever. At the very height of the summer season in 1948, Jack was seriously hurt. Jack was a man of action, and he loved to be surrounded with people and activity. Some of his favorite things were horseback riding, speedboating, sailing, and aquaplaning. One day when he was out on his aquaplane in the middle of Schroon Lake, he hit the wake of another speedboat and went flying into the air and then crashed hard back into the water.

As soon as Jack hit the water, he knew he was seriously hurt; all he could do was try to hold on until help came. When his rescuers arrived and pulled him out of the water to put him in the speedboat, he nearly passed out from the pain. He was then rushed to a doctor and on to the local hospital. A very rapid examination discovered that Jack had broken his hip. Since there were few facilities in the Adirondacks at that time, an ambulance was not available, and Jack had to be taken to New Jersey in a hearse. Marge sat alongside him all the way, as Jack endured excruciating pain. In his heart he was wondering, "Why, Lord?

In the midst of such tremendous blessing, why did this have to happen? What would happen to the camp? What would happen to all the young people at the Island? The radio program? The radio rallies? What would happen?"

Some people get discouraged in the midst of trial and testing and give up, but Jack was exactly the opposite. He showed his very best when the odds were against him. When he arrived at the hospital, he was informed by the medical personnel that he would be hospitalized from four to six months, but God took over in a wonderful way. A very serious operation was performed, during which a Vitallium pin was driven through the joint fracture. Within a week Jack was trying out his crutches. Jack stayed in the hospital for two weeks, and during that time did two of his Saturday night coast-to-coast broadcasts right from his hospital room. Within two weeks Jack was back at camp, directing everything, giving orders, praying with people, counseling, preaching, and serving God on his crutches. Jack knew and served the living God, Who is still in the miracle business. He enabled Jack under all circumstances to come through for His honor and glory.

The camp program on Word of Life Island is unbelievable with activities happening all the time. It is a place where young people come alive... sports, social activity, concerts, banquets, and, of course, tremendous meetings with great men of God to instruct the campers in the Word of God.

M.A. Butler, the former director of the ministry of Word of Life in Australia, remembers going to camp: "It all started in June 1961, while driving alone in Ohio on Route 14. I tuned the radio to a station and heard a West Point cadet giving a testimony about the Lord Jesus Christ. Then an enthusiastic guy came on telling of an island with all its thrills and romances. 'You write for a folder,' he said, and I did. This was the beginning. I set foot on the Island in August 1961. It was that night my thoughts were directed to the Word of God, the Bible. I was shown how Jesus Christ came from the glories of Heaven to die on the cross for my sins. I was shown how He conquered death and arose from the grave.

I was shown how if I, M.A. Butler, believed that Jesus Christ did this for me, I would be a child of God. Yes, that first night on Word of Life Island I became a child of God, and, truly, life was new. I hadn't told my parents where I was going, and after sending them a postcard, I told them I was at Word of Life Island. They thought I was at a nudist camp. When I returned home, my mother found a pastor and asked him about her son who had gone off on a religious kick. The following year, however, I joined the Island staff. That year my 14-year-old brother was saved at the Island with 18 others from my hometown. In January 1963, God led me to a great Christian school. During this time, I saw my mother, a sister-in-law, and my grandfather, on his deathbed, all come to the Savior. In 1966 God gave me a Christian girl for my wife – where else, but on the Island!"

In 1953 a problem began bothering Word of Life again – growing pains. It seemed that whatever Jack put his hand to God blessed in a remarkable way. Now a lot of young people were growing up, and they wanted to come back to camp with their families. The young people wanted to bring their mothers and fathers, their little brothers and sisters, but the Island was just for young people.

For many years, Jack used to look from the Island over to the mainland and see the beautiful, exclusive Brown Swan Club. Could that possibly be a place for an adult camp? One day Jack and some members of the Board of Directors were on their knees in prayer. While they were praying, God spoke to the heart of Leon Sullivan, a Christian businessman who is now with the Lord. Leon was a faithful friend to Word of Life and close personal friend to Jack. When they had finished praying, he said, "Jack, I feel that I should go over to the Brown Swan and speak to the man who owns it. I believe the Lord is leading us in that direction."

Within a few moments, Mr. Sullivan was in the boat on his way to the Brown Swan Club. As he walked into the main lobby he met the owner, Mr. Greenberg, and told him he wanted to buy the place. Mr. Greenberg took one look at him and said, "Mr. Sullivan, we wouldn't sell you the place for a million dollars."

Leon looked at him and said, "Thank you, we don't want to buy it for a million dollars because we don't have that kind of money."

One year later the group met again on the Island. Once again, they were praying about the possibility of getting the Brown Swan Club. When they finished praying, Mr. Sullivan said, "Jack, I'm going to try it again!"

The following day, after much prayer, Leon Sullivan and his wife started across the lake in an open boat, full of confidence that it was God's will they make a new proposal. It was a rainy day, and by the time they arrived, they were both drenched. As they walked into the lobby of the Club, the owner's first impression was that they were out of work and looking for jobs as dishwashers. He barked at Leon and said, "What do you want?"

"I want to buy the place!" Leon shouted back.

The man said, "Come in; how much do you want to pay?" Leon began to tell him how they had had the prayer meeting and how God had moved upon his heart to come over and speak to him. He told him how the Island was for young people and that they needed a place for adults. He said, "I know, Mr. Greenberg, that you wanted a million dollars a year ago. We don't have that kind of money, but I am prepared to make an offer, and I would like to explain that we have no desire to be unfair with you. But frankly, it's all that Jack Wyrtzen feels the Lord has told him to pay."

Mr. Greenberg literally shot back, "Okay, let's hear it."

About 25 feet from where Mr. Sullivan was talking there was a man playing the piano with a big cigar hanging out of the side of his mouth and a girl dancing around him in the familiar garb of a nightclub entertainer. People were drinking and even as Mr. Sullivan looked at Mr. Greenberg, he thought, "Oh, God, if you can move this man's heart in this place where sin is abounding, may the grace of God abound even more, and may this be the place where many people come to know and love the Savior."

He looked at Mr. Greenberg and said, "Here's our proposal. May I say you can keep all your cigars, cigarettes, the bar, liquor, the cash register and everything you regard as personal. We're not interested in any of that. We want the linens, silverware, furniture, equipment – in fact, everything needed to run the place, for which, Mr. Greenberg, I am instructed to offer you $125,000 in cash."

Leon was certain that Mr. Greenberg would say, "I would not even consider that! Your price is far too low!" The piano was playing; the girl was dancing. Leon was praying, and he knew that back on Word of Life Island a whole group was praying with him. Leon stood up and said, "Mr. Greenberg, here's my card. Mrs. Sullivan and I are leaving for Philadelphia right now, and if you find you can accept the bid, please call me."

As soon as Leon and Mrs. Sullivan were in the car, they bowed their heads and prayed that God would perform a miracle in Mr. Greenberg's life. Leon called up Jack and said, "Just keep praying; I am sure something is going to happen."

The next morning Leon was at his office desk scarcely an hour when Jack called and literally screamed on the phone. "Guess what, Leon! Mr. Greenberg has accepted our offer of $125,000! Praise the Lord! Praise the Lord!" Truly, it was nothing less than a miracle, for it was all of God. Actually, Mr. Greenberg had said to Jack, "Wyrtzen, you know, if Mr. Sullivan had come one day sooner or one day later, you would not have been able to buy the Club. You see, the very day he came, my cook had quit, and I was sick and tired of all the problems of running the Brown Swan, so I said to my wife, 'If anyone comes in and wants to buy the place, I'll give it to them.'" Yes, praise God, miracles do take place!

Now another miracle was necessary – $125,000 cash. Where could it come from? Jack began to pray. In just 30 days the money was in – $50,000 from friends and $75,000 from mortgages. The Brown Swan Club became the Word of Life Inn. Settlement was planned for October 15, but as God would have it, the closing happened on August 15 which meant that Word of Life could host a Bible conference the last two weeks of August and over the Labor Day weekend. When Jack told this to Mr. Sullivan, Leon bowed his head, stood there, and cried like a baby. Now Word of Life was not only an Island for teenagers in the middle of Schroon Lake but also the Word of Life Inn for adults.

However, soon the same problem showed up once again – growing pains. Word of Life had the Island for teenagers and the Inn for adults, but they now needed a camp to take care of boys and girls. Early in 1954 Jack had been invited to see another beautiful piece of property, also on Schroon Lake. It consisted of 135 acres of land, 28 modern buildings, a beautiful beach, a large theater, a brand-new dining room, several fine tennis courts, and, in addition to all this, there were stables, canoes, rowboats, a basketball court, and a baseball field. Jack took time to look at only half of the property. He stopped and right there bowed his head, "Lord, is this the place we're looking for?" This was far beyond anything he could ever have dreamed of obtaining for Word of Life, a Ranch for boys and girls.

He turned to the owner and said, "How much do you want for it?"

The owner said, "I've invested $300,000 into this place, but I'm willing to let it go a lot cheaper. I need $170,000." Jack got back to his office at the Island. Soon he was on the telephone calling the Board of Directors and the Council. Together they prayed about it, and, as they prayed, Jack felt a strong conviction that it would have to be, once again, on a miracle basis. This was the only way they could possibly hope to get it. God told Jack what he should offer the man for the property.

In just a little while, he was down at the campsite once again. Facing the owner, he began, "After much prayer I feel that we should offer you

$60,000 for the place and no more – not even $60,001." After some careful thinking, the owner slowly rose to his feet and shook hands with Jack. When he said, "Jack, I want you to have the place, and I'm accepting your offer of $60,000," Jack just about fell over. God had worked another miracle; it was Word of Life Ranch, a paradise for boys and girls that was a success right from the very opening.

Jack was serious about wise Christian stewardship and felt a responsibility to get maximum use from the resources God had given him. The Ranch buildings were winterized, so why should they be used only during the summer and remain vacant the other three seasons of the year? In 1970 the facilities were put to use year round when the Word of Life Bible Institute was established – and later a Snow Camp was started which today runs every winter weekend from mid-January through mid-March. The Bible Institute grew to a college campus for nearly 500 students, and the Word of Life Ranch was relocated to an adjacent property acquired in 1973.

Two years later, another nearby property was purchased for the Word of Life Family Campground, with housekeeping cottages and campsites for nearly 100 recreational vehicles, campers, trailers, or tents. The Campground features a private lake, outdoor swimming pool, indoor and outdoor sports facilities, snack shack and auditorium – and has been a great success due to its fine facilities and the growing popularity of camping.

Over the years, the facilities at the Word of Life Inn have undergone several expansions. Today there is an 800-seat auditorium, a bookstore and gift shop, a miniature golf course, volleyball court, and shuffleboard. During the 1970's, the construction of the Chalets and the William's Motel added to the number of available rooms. In 1982, the Conference Center was opened. The Center features a plush grand lobby, 105 luxurious rooms, a beautiful indoor heated pool, whirlpool, saunas, and game rooms. Easily the finest and most modern Christian conference facility in the Northeast, the Center has allowed Word of Life to expand its adult programs. In addition to summer conferences, Word of Life hosts Fall Foliage weekends and specialty-themed conferences throughout the year.

Today the combined attendance at Word of Life camps each year is some 20,000. The miracle is not only the great numbers who come but the great numbers who have received the Lord as their Savior, while thousands of others have been challenged to go into full-time service.

CHAPTER 9

The Windows

Where there is no vision, the people perish..
Proverbs 29:18 KJV

It was another great Saturday night Word of Life youth rally. Jack Wyrtzen had finished preaching and was giving an invitation for missionary service, while staff pianist, Harry Bollback, was at the keyboard playing the invitation song. The needs of a lost world had been plainly presented, but as Jack started to lead one last chorus of the invitation hymn, there was no piano accompaniment. The capacity audience which had jammed the auditorium continued to sing, but Jack looked wonderingly at the piano. To his surprise Harry Bollback was no longer there but was walking to the front to join the many others who were dedicating their lives to full-time Christian service.

Jack took seriously the Scriptural admonition to "provoke one another unto good works." When he saw someone who was available, he urged that person to use his talents for the Lord. Harry was only 16 when he volunteered to play the piano at a Word of Life prison meeting, but Jack at once recognized his abilities, and in 1941 invited the young man to play full time.

Six years later, when God called Harry to the mission field, Jack never thought about the musical talent Word of Life was losing. Instead, as a Board Member of the South American Indian Mission, Jack shared with Harry the tremendous needs of that continent and encouraged Harry to go. Stirred by God's calling and Jack's vision, Harry enrolled in Bible College and in 1950 departed with his family for the wilds of central Brazil.

Along with his colleague, Harold Reimer, Harry invested four years of his life among some of the most savage Indians of the 20th century. Perhaps the two missionaries' most daring and rewarding exploit was to seek out and contact the fierce Xavante tribe. These Indians massacred any white men who came near. For several days and nights, Harry and his companions were chased downstream by the maddened Indians, but because of the width of the river and God's providence, the arrows shot at their canoe always missed the intended targets.

After their escape, an even greater miracle happened. The very same Indians who had pursued the missionary team, later walked into the base camp on the edge of the jungle where Harry and his family were living. This time it was a peaceful contact; a contact that grew. Today among the Xavante Indians of Brazil there are scores of Christians. Some of the very same men who tried to kill Harry and Harold are now pastors of churches among their own people – and their grandchildren are studying at the Word of Life Bible Institute in Brazil to become missionaries themselves!

Toward the end of their term in 1955, Harry and Harold were invited by Jack Wyrtzen to attend a series of meetings Jack was conducting in Brazil. The three met at a little town in the Brazilian state of Mato Grosso. It was a night of great festivity, for a new electrical system was just being installed, and thousands of townspeople were in the streets with fireworks, bands, enthusiasm, and excitement. In the midst of all this, Jack turned to Harry and said, "Just think, if we could harness all that enthusiasm for the Lord. What an impact it would make! You know, I believe it would be great if we could get a Word of Life camp started for the youth in Brazil."

Shortly thereafter, the Bollbacks returned to the United States on furlough and came to Schroon Lake. The needs of Brazilian youth had been burned into Harry's soul, and so he reminded Jack of his comment in Mato Grosso. "Why couldn't God do the same thing with the youth of Brazil as He was doing through Word of Life in the United States?" If God could use the ministry of Word of Life in hundreds and thousands of young people's lives through rallies and camps in the United States, why couldn't He do it in Brazil?

Windows in a house serve a twofold purpose... to bring light in and allow occupants to look out. Living in a dark room is depressing. Plants and flowers cannot grow in the dark; they need light. With windows, you can look out and become aware of things taking place. You can see. You can gain a vision. That is why the Bible says, Where there is no vision, the people perish. The Lord said, Lift up your eyes. So, Jack, Harry and Harold began to meet at 6:00 a.m. every Wednesday at Word of Life Island to pray about the possibility of starting a youth camp in Brazil. One Wednesday morning Harry Bollback said, "Lord, if you want Harold and I to go back to Brazil and start a Word of Life camp, then give us a sign today." When they were finished, Jack said, "If camping is in God's plan for Brazil, He will surely give you a go-ahead sign."

It was still Wednesday morning. Harry went over to the Word of Life Inn to play the piano. At the entrance to the auditorium a lady told Harry that God had burdened her heart since Sunday for Brazil. She knew nothing of the prayer meeting or the possibility of a camp. She just wanted to help the Word of Life ministry in Brazil with a check for $100. Then that afternoon a man came up to Harry and said, "I'd like to talk to you about Brazil." They spoke together a few moments, and then Harry left for the dining room to eat. But before he could bow his head and thank the Lord for the meal, one of the waiters brought over a little envelope. Inside was a $500 check from the man Harry had been talking with earlier.

Harry ran to the telephone. "Jack, maybe you're used to receiving $600 in one day, but I'm not!"

"Praise the Lord," Jack exclaimed. "God has given you His sign to go ahead with the Word of Life camp in Brazil."

Soon another 6:00 a.m. prayer meeting was held in the boathouse at

Word of Life Island. The vision of a new work in Brazil was placed before the members of the Word of Life Board. Jack closed the meeting with everyone singing, "Great is Thy Faithfulness." In that moment in 1957, Word of Life became "Word of Life International."

When Harry and Harold returned to Brazil with their families that year, it was not to the green jungles of the wild but to the concrete jungles of the huge city of Sao Paulo. There were many obstacles to overcome as the two men had little money and had contacts only with the Indians. The pair filled their suitcases with Gospels and boarded a bus. But to where? They knew no one. They prayed, "God, lead us to a town where we can conduct evangelistic meetings." Stopping in the village of Atibaia, they got off the old bus. There was a man standing on the street corner. "Sir, sir... excuse me," said Harry in Portuguese. "Could you tell me if there is an evangelical church in this area? We are missionaries from North America and want to conduct some evangelistic meetings."

The Brazilian man on the street began to weep. Bewildered, Harry and Harold asked, "Why the tears?" The reply came, "I am a pastor in this country, and for six months my people and I have been praying sincerely that God would send someone to us to conduct some meetings. Even now I was just praying for this, but I did not expect it to happen quite this way!"

Those meetings were highly successful, and many were saved. Through the support and encouragement of a growing number of believers who shared the vision of a camp for Brazilian young people, within a year Word of Life was able to purchase a beautiful valley in a small town outside Sao Paulo. However, there were no roads into the valley, so they had to be made. There was no electricity, so a hydroelectric plant had to be constructed and electrical power lines installed before opening to eleven campers that first week of summer camp in 1958.

Improvements were made throughout the next year as an artificial lake was created by damming a stream on the property. Surrounded by a lush green forest, the lake was truly a focal point for the whole camp setting. But as camp was about to open in 1959, the dam burst after an unusually ferocious tropical rainstorm, leaving a huge mudhole in the middle of camp instead of a beautiful lake. The staff who had labored so hard and faithfully to prepare for a successful camping season were overwhelmed with discouragement. But it was not long before the discouragement gave way to song as Harry penned the words and music: "Ring the bells, ring the bells, let the whole world know; Christ the Savior lives today, as He did so long ago."

The Brazilian camp began on a miracle basis and still prospers today in a miraculous way, first under the leadership of Harold Reimer, followed today by the leadership of his son, John. Attendance has grown from 300 young people that first summer in 1958 to more than 13,000 each year who spend a week of their lives at "Palavra da Vida." Hundreds upon hundreds have found Christ as their Savior, and many are training at the Brazilian Word of Life Bible Institute, begun in 1965, to reach out around South America and the world as missionaries and pastors.

Still told is the story of Lau Gomes, who came to camp in the summer of 1964. Earlier that year, when the military took over Brazil, Lau was sent to prison. He was a Communist, an agitator, and a leader of a Maoist youth organization. After his release from jail, it seemed everything went from bad to worse. No more political discussions were allowed, and all his political friends were afraid to associate with him because the Communist Party had been outlawed. He had difficulty making new friends because people didn't want to be associated with a Communist. When Lau got into a fight one day, he was taken to the hospital. Someone there suggested, "When you get out, how about going to Palavra da Vida?" Lau had often heard about Palavra da Vida through friends who were active in the Bible Clubs in Sao Paulo, but they were Christians, and he had no intention of joining them. "However," he thought, "they're not the worst people. Perhaps the camp would be a good place to get my mind off my troubles." Soon Lau was on his way by bus. At the camp entrance he was met by his counselor. The camp was centered around a picturesque lake and swaying trees, beautifully set in a valley. Everyone seemed to be having a great time. But when Lau heard that besides morning quiet time and evening devotions there were two Bible studies each day, he was ready to leave!

One morning Lau got up early while the sun was still low. He looked over the countryside and said to himself, "God, will you just show me how I can know you?" A few days later, led by his caring counselor, Lau came to know Jesus Christ as his Savior. Lau was inexperienced with the Word of God, but he had read about Saul, his conversion on the road to Damascus, and how the one-time destroyer of the church became its great builder. In a testimony meeting the day Lau was saved, he looked at the young people and said, "Most of you don't know me. Until 15 minutes ago, I was just like Saul. But now I want to be like Paul." He sat down. Nobody understood what he was talking about. "Stand up and tell us more," they said. So, Lau continued to tell how he had received the Lord as his Savior.

Later, Lau worked several years on the camp staff and then graduated from the Palavra da Vida Bible Institute for missionary service, witnessing to other Brazilian young people of the peace that comes through knowing Jesus Christ as personal Savior.

Characteristically, the Word of Life overseas ministries were not started through any prior plan made by men. As the Lord opened doors, Jack recognized and had the vision to act upon these opportunities. Jack never intended to establish a camping ministry, Bible Clubs, or a Bible Institute – nor did he set out with the intention to expand Word of Life into other nations. But God said in Jeremiah 29:11, *For I know the thoughts that I think toward you, saith the Lord, thoughts of peace, and not of evil, to give you an expected end.* Today, Word of Life Brazil celebrates more than 60 years of abundant ministry, yet Harry Bollback and Harold Reimer initially went to that country as missionaries for another Christian organization to evangelize the jungle Indians, never even thinking about a camp or Bible Institute for city youth.

An unforeseen opportunity knocked again in 1965, even as Word of Life marked its 25th anniversary. At that time, Word of Life considered itself a domestic organization which also happened to have a project in the single country of Brazil. Most men would be satisfied with the ministry Jack already had. The house was already big; actually, the house was enormous and the budget tremendous. The house already had enough windows... or did it?

Four young men who had graduated together from Canada's Briercrest Bible College needed help. Bob Parschauer, Larry Locken, Chuck Kosman and Len Wiebe were bound for Germany as missionary candidates with the Greater Europe Mission but were experiencing difficulty raising financial support. Jack learned about their trouble, and, having heard the four sing as a gospel quartet, took them on his speaking tour for a year. Soon their support was raised, and the four Canadians were off to Germany. But, while on the field, the men felt God was not leading them to split up and join various church-planting teams as the mission agency intended. Instead, they believed the Lord wanted them together in an evangelistic ministry. They called Jack Wyrtzen about their dilemma.

"Why don't you come with Word of Life," Jack suggested, "and start a youth camp in Germany?"

For the next four years, the quartet rented facilities in different European countries and conducted Word of Life camps for young people, but they were never able to find a permanent campsite. Land is very scarce in Germany, for the country is approximately equal in size to the state of Oregon. Yet, in a wonderful way, God performed another miracle and gave Word of Life Germany a beautiful castle just outside the city of Munich. On June 12, 1969, Word of Life's German camp was dedicated to the glory of God.

When the quartet received the castle, it needed substantial funds to make many needed repairs. One day, a large truck began to unload paint in front of the castle. The Word of Life staff was very concerned.

They didn't have any money. They checked – nobody had ordered paint. They spoke to the man who was unloading the paint and told him, "We're very sorry, sir, but there must be a mistake. Nobody here ordered any paint. Besides, we don't have any money to pay for it even though the castle desperately needs a paint job."

The man, however, kept unloading the paint. When he finished, he said, "There's a Christian businessman in town who feels the castle needs to be painted inside and out. He sent the paint free of charge so the building could look better."

The truck pulled away, but soon another truck arrived. The driver began to unload rugs and linoleum. Another Christian businessman in Germany was giving Word of Life approximately $1,800 worth of rugs and linoleum! Since that very humble beginning, God has blessed in a remarkable way. From all over Europe, young people came. Soon the castle was not large enough; more space was needed, and God performed another miracle. On Lake Starnberg, just a few minutes' walk from the castle, there was another large 100-room castle. Jack suggested the quartet get in touch with the authorities and explore the possibility of acquiring these facilities. It seemed impossible. Money was too scarce. But through a series of circumstances that could only have been superintended by God Himself, Word of Life obtained a contract to rent the new castle for only $25 per month!

The way God was blessing in Brazil and Germany caused Harry Bollback to write to Jack Wyrtzen. Harry suggested that Word of Life should get camps started in many countries around the world. Jack wrote back, "Praise the Lord – great idea! Let's pray about it." Soon Harry laid down a plan for Jack, showing how Word of Life could get ten camps started in ten years. Everyone thought it was a terrific plan.

The following Sunday, Jack Wyrtzen called. "Harry, I'm getting all the staff together to go over the plans for overseas camping, but we have changed the goal. We are not aiming for ten camps any longer."

"What are we aiming for now?" Harry asked.

Jack replied, "Well, I'm going to tell the young people we are aiming for 100 camps in the next ten years."

"How could we possibly do it?" Harry thought to himself. But instead, he told Jack, "I'll be flying up and seeing you at camp in a few days, and we'll go over it together." Later, as Harry was traveling to Schroon Lake, he went over in his mind the foolishness of trying to start 100 camps in ten years. As soon as he met Jack at camp, Jack said, "Harry, do you remember that number I gave you over the phone the other day?"

Harry remembered it well, and replied, "Yes, I do." "It's the wrong number," continued Jack.

"Praise the Lord," exclaimed Harry. "I'm glad you realize that." "We're going to make it 200 instead of 100!" declared Jack.

This is vision! This is what has made Word of Life move! In 1969, Harry returned to the home office as Word of Life Co-Director to head up the new overseas ministries – and things began to happen! Jack had a vision of a worldwide ministry, and, within three years, Word of Life had established camps on all six inhabited continents. First, Brazil and Germany, and then over the years new windows were opened in more countries such as Australia, Ecuador, Kenya, Philippines, Argentina, Japan, Venezuela, Portugal, Spain, Chile, Uruguay, New Zealand, Fiji, Mexico, Costa Rica, Netherlands Antilles, Colombia, Peru, Paraguay, England, Italy, Hungary, Poland, Canada and many more. The opening of each country has been a story of God's grace and goodness, and stories continue to be told as the camps reach out to more than 100,000 young people each year worldwide.

For example, from Argentina comes a story that began almost 50 years ago in Lakeland, Florida. Don Kelso was 35 years of age and a successful businessman. His good friend, city magistrate, Jim Welch, had a "religious experience," and Don went to ask about it. After hearing the Gospel clearly presented, Don accepted the Lord a few days later in Jim's office.

A year later Don helped organize some local meetings where Jack Wyrtzen preached. Jack challenged Don to help support a young missionary named Paul Bubar, who was starting the first Word of Life Bible Club in central Florida. Don accepted the challenge, and as the ministry of Bible Clubs grew, Don began organizing bus trips to Word of Life Island in Schroon Lake for young people from central Florida.

One year, because the bus Don had chartered broke down, he was forced to shop around for another bus for the camp trip. The substitute bus had ten additional seats. Not wanting to waste the space, Don began looking for ten additional campers. One of the campers he found was an eighth-grade boy with a bad home situation. The boy was in trouble with the law, and under the terms of his probation could not leave the state without permission. Don approached the legal authorities to make the necessary arrangements, and in God's providence the magistrate turned out to be none other than Jim Welch! Permission was granted, and the young troublemaker, Joe Jordan, was saved that week on Word of Life Island.

Joe later attended Bible school and became burdened for the young people of Argentina. In 1970 he began the ministry of Word of Life there. Beto Tarasiuk was one of the first people Joe met in Argentina. Beto was a professional soccer player, but he wanted to learn how to play American basketball. A relationship was formed, and in the following years, Beto served with Word of Life in Paraguay, Italy and Chile.

Dan Nuesch attended the very first camping session in Argentina and was saved. He gave up his nightclub job and ultimately became the Co-Director of Word of Life Argentina.

Disc jockey, Manolo Gomez, and construction worker, Tito Pagano, attended Joe Jordan's first Bible Club. Manolo has served with Word of Life in Colombia and Argentina, while Tito has ministered in Chile and El Salvador.

Leo DiGilio, a former drug addict, directs the Word of Life Camps in Mexico. Other products of Joe Jordan's ministry include the current directors of the work of Word of Life in almost every Spanish-speaking country in Latin America.

But there's more to this story!

Ten years after Harry Bollback returned to the home office as Word of Life Co-Director, the overseas ministry was being carried on by scores of able and dedicated Christians around the world. Harry had gradually assumed more duties throughout the organization, and in 1979 relinquished day-to-day management of the Overseas Department to Don

Kelso! During Don's eight years in the post, the number of American and National missionaries on the Word of Life support rolls grew from 60 to 260. So, there was a need to coordinate furloughs, define recruitment and training standards, and address many other administrative tasks required for a large international organization to function effectively. When Don retired in 1987, the man appointed director of the Word of Life overseas ministries was none other than Paul Bubar – whom Don Kelso had first supported as a new missionary some 28 years before!

"Why have Word of Life overseas ministries grown so much and been so fruitful?" asks Don Kelso. "Some of it has to do with our philosophy and methods. In today's world economy, people in every country are flocking to the cities – and we try to locate our camps near cities. Half of our camps are in predominantly Catholic countries, yet parents let their children attend camp because it's better than the streets. Also, two-thirds of our overseas staff are not Americans. More than half of our Word of Life fields are directed by non-Americans. People from America are well liked in some countries and less liked in others, but in all countries, gaining acceptance is usually easier when Word of Life is not perceived as a totally American program directed from abroad.

However, any explanation of Word of Life's growth overseas has to go back to Jack's tremendous vision and personal love for missions. Busy as he was, Jack fell in love with every Word of Life missionary. He gave them money from his own pocket and made it a personal project to promote their support. He helped put them in touch with good people who could assist them financially. For example, if missionaries were home on furlough, Jack would take them to dinner at the Word of Life Inn and then make sure all the 'right' people were invited to sit at their table. Jack was so missions-minded and world-minded, that he took a personal interest in every missionary he ever met."

Jack Wyrtzen was constantly asking God for new windows in the house through which to look out and see those lost and needy souls. He would never be satisfied with simply a local ministry. Nor did Jack operate through consolidation – but only through expansion, reaching out to the far corners of the earth. One of the great reasons for the success of the ministry of Word of Life overseas is that Jack gathered around him persons of like-mindedness who were concerned about one thing – looking out and reaching people with the Gospel. Jack had total confidence in the men who were sent out to get the job done. Jack's great desire he had from the day he dedicated his life to the Lord was finally being realized – the desire to multiply himself spiritually. Perhaps it was not done in the way he originally anticipated, but Jack never questioned for a moment that when God said, Delight thyself also in the Lord, and He shall give thee the desires of thine heart, God meant it!

CHAPTER 10

The Yard

*Come, you children, listen to me;
I will teach you the fear of the LORD. Psalm 34:11*

Jack Wyrtzen believed in the local, Bible-believing church as God's program for today. Jack has said, "Organizations like Word of Life will come and go; history has proven this. But the local church, the true body of believers in Christ, will go on. Therefore, we had better build into God's program." For this reason, Word of Life has always been a branch of evangelism for the local, Bible-believing church.

Evangelism with Jack took on many forms… he was not afraid of something new. Although he was cautious, he moved quickly when he was sure. Usually new ideas did not begin with Jack. He heard and listened much more than most people realize. He heard something, wrote it down (he always had plenty of paper and red ink pens), and then began to pray. Sometime later, he would say, "You know, the other day I was thinking about this, and I came up with a great idea." The great idea was often what somebody suggested to him sometime before – but once it became Jack's idea, things moved fast.

He expected everyone to go at the same pace he went – which was unending go, go, go! Jack couldn't understand why it should take three days to get a job done. In fact, he felt any job, regardless of how involved it was, should be completed in one day and sometimes in half an hour.

It was Jack's drive and motivation to get out the message of the Gospel which did this. The details didn't concern him; he let others handle them. This question of detail showed up even in his home. His daughter, Betsy, says, "He was impractical. He may have had a big vision for getting housework done, so long as everyone else did it. But he just didn't realize the details involved."

Others remember a story from the first year camp opened at Word of Life. An old barn that had been unoccupied for a long time was to be used by the staff. The dirt was nearly an inch thick, and it all had to be cleaned. Jack arrived on the scene to show the clean-up crew how to do the job, and for the next five minutes, dust was scattered in every direction. Nobody could even stay in the room. Jack said, "Now that is how it should be done" – and left!

Since the day he met the Savior, Jack Wyrtzen had one goal and purpose in life... to reach as many people with the Gospel as he could in the shortest amount of time possible. This gave him a zest for living and for reaching young people, from the time he gave his life to Jesus Christ at age nineteen until he went Home to be with the Lord.

Jack had a heart for young people... a desire to reach as many as possible, as soon as possible, with the Gospel... a commitment to the local, Bible-believing church... impatience with details... and a cautious approach to new ideas but fast action when the concept took hold. Nowhere are these facets of Jack's character better illustrated than in the story of how Word of Life Bible Clubs – which today reach thousands of young people on a weekly basis in several hundred churches across the country – were first established.

The idea started with a young missionary, Paul Bubar, who in 1956 was working with another youth organization in Florida. Things were not going well. There was too much compromise. In fact, one day Paul asked, "Lord, why in the world did you bring me to this place?" Paul felt he could no longer continue in his position. He noticed that Jack Wyrtzen was holding some meetings in the Florida area and determined to go hear the famous youth evangelist. He listened one night as Jack preached from 1 Corinthians on the kind of men God can use. Not many mighty, not many noble are called: but God hath chosen the foolish... the weak... the base... to bring to nought things that are. God was speaking to him. "That's me," Paul said. Right then and there he rededicated his life to the Lord. "Anything, any place, anytime; here I am."

That meeting was a turning point in Paul Bubar's life. However, for Jack Wyrtzen the significance was certainly not immediately obvious. Paul spoke to Jack about the possibility of starting Word of Life Bible Clubs, but Jack said, "Nothing doing; we already have enough irons in the fire. We can't keep up with what God has given us already. There just doesn't seem to be a possibility right now." Jack wasn't interested. How could he be? Word of Life was expanding at such a rate that to consider something new would be impossible... or would it? The words "slow down" were not in Jack's vocabulary.

But the idea was now in Jack's mind, and as he began to pray about Bible Clubs over a two-year period, God put the whole picture together. The more he thought it over, the more Jack was convinced of the need for a grassroots program for teenagers – not just one-night or extended crusades but a solid and lasting work that could help young people in a local church situation. The time was right, so in 1959, Word of Life Bible Clubs were born.

Jack called Paul Bubar to see if he was still interested in coming to Schroon Lake to head up the operation. Paul was ready! Next, someone was needed in Florida to direct the first club on site, and a young Word of Life camp counselor named George Theis was sent. George later went to the mission field with Word of Life in Brazil and in 1983 rejoined the home staff as Co-Director.

Today, Word of Life area missionaries across the United States and Canada work with Club leaders in each church, training them in leadership and evangelism skills, doctrine, discipleship, time management, goal setting, and personal Christian living.

Word of Life Bible Clubs are designed for youth of all ages beginning with the Early Learners program for the Preschool and Kindergarten age, followed by the Olympian program for ages 6-13 and Teen Clubs for both Junior and Senior High students. These clubs are sponsored by Bible-believing churches throughout North America, and each year thousands of salvation and dedication decisions are recorded through this dynamic Word of Life program.

Jack Wyrtzen used every means available to achieve his desire for reaching as many people as possible in the shortest time with the Gospel. For that reason, new rooms and additions have constantly been added to the house. A home needs a yard where the youngsters can play and exercise, grow and learn under family supervision, and invite their friends to share in that joy. In just that way, Word of Life Bible Clubs provide young people the means, the room, and the guidance to grow to spiritual maturity in an environment of love and concern – and as Jack would heartily agree, even fun!

CHAPTER 11

The Guest Room

Be hospitable to one another... 1 Peter 4:9

Because Word of Life touches so many thousands of lives, each year of ministry brings its own special blessings as God continues to prosper the work around the world. It is difficult, therefore, to single out which years are "important" to the organization's history. But 1969 stands out as a year in which several milestone events came together and launched Word of Life into new and unforeseen directions.

Harry Bollback was called back from Brazil by Jack Wyrtzen to join the home staff as Co-Director and to head up a new Overseas Department. Word of Life Bible Clubs celebrated their tenth year with thousands of young people involved throughout the land. The phenomenal growth of Word of Life camping programs, already more than 20 years old, necessitated permanent relocation of the Headquarters offices to Schroon Lake.

In fact, Word of Life Overseas Ministries and Bible Clubs were growing at such a rate that a new need developed – the need for a place to train and prepare Christian young people to become leaders.

Jack always enjoyed being around people... working with them, helping them, and training them. How could he do it? He was already involved in so many ministries with Word of Life. Could he be stretched a little more?

By this time, Word of Life Brazil had started a Bible Institute under the direction of Jack's son-in-law, Dave Cox. Already, the school was training young Brazilians for Christian service, using a unique three-part program that stressed academics, attitude, and practice. So, it's not surprising that one day someone said to Jack, "What you need in America is a Bible School."

"A Bible School! That's the last thing Word of Life is interested in. Besides, there are a lot of good schools already doing the job." But the seed was planted. Jack was praying... thinking... planning. At the Word of Life Ranch, many buildings were already winterized but used only during the summer. Why couldn't the Ranch buildings be used the rest of the year for a school – a Bible School?

For every job there must be a man. If Word of Life was planning a school, then the Lord had to send the right man to direct it. Several years earlier Paul Brownback, a cadet at West Point, had met Jack when he was conducting Bible classes at the military school. Paul was a young man with a vibrant testimony. As a cadet, he traveled around with Jack in meetings, giving his testimony and playing his trumpet. Later, Paul was sent to Vietnam and then on to Germany, where he met the Word of Life team there and was a great help to the ministry in that country. Paul felt down deep in his heart that God was leading him out of the service of his country and into service for the Lord, so he left the military to attend seminary.

Jack Wyrtzen hadn't even thought about a Bible Institute, but God had – and He was already fitting the pieces together. By September of 1970, everything had come together – the need, the vision, the facilities, and the man – and so the Word of Life Bible Institute was born. When the Institute opened that month, instead of the 50 students expected, 73 arrived. The following year Word of Life planned to host 100 students, but the Lord sent 126! Today more 550 students from nearly every state and more than 20 countries attend first and second-year programs at Word of Life Bible Institute campuses in New York and in Florida.

The Institute offers an absolutely unique program where students are trained in the Word of God and also in practical ministry. Whether the student's objective is to go on to finish a four-year college to prepare for full-time Christian service or to enter a secular career, Word of Life believes every Christian can benefit from setting aside time to become grounded in God's Word. The goal of all Word of Life schools is to help students develop spiritually so their lives might be ones of maximum effectiveness for the Lord. In so doing, the Bible Institute program emphasizes three keys to building in each student a firm foundation for Christian character... a profound working knowledge of the Word of God, a disciplined life, and the ability to influence the lives of others for God. Since its inception, Word of Life Bible Institute has graduated thousands of men and women of all ages, many of whom have gone on to full- time ministry with Word of Life or other Christian organizations. Each student has a unique and important story, each precious to our Lord Jesus Christ. To demonstrate the Christ-like character and commitment the Institute strives to instill in each student, Jack Wyrtzen liked to tell the deeply moving story of Jay Butcher who graduated from the Bible Institute in 1983.

Born into a family with parents who loved the Lord, Jay was taught God's Word at an early age. His family lived in Washington State. Jay's father was a farmer who often worked late into the evenings, yet his mother did not allow this fact to excuse a neglect of family devotions. God honored the testimony of this godly mother and gave her the joy of leading her son at the age of five to give his heart to Jesus.

Strong and athletic, Jay became a top high school wrestler. Unfortunately, his spiritual life was not characterized by the same discipline as his athletic pursuits. Jay struggled in living for the Lord as a teenager but as a high school senior decided to become active in his church youth program. He even took an interest in singing, something Jay had resisted before. At the young people's group, Jay met a friend who encouraged him to consider Word of Life Bible Institute after graduation. Jay and his parents prayed for God's leading, and the Lord opened the way for Jay to enroll at the Institute in the fall of 1982. Soon he joined the Collegians and traveled throughout the United States and even to Great Britain in presenting one of Word of Life's musical dramas, "The Revelation." "Isn't it great to know that whatever happens, God is in control," Jay wrote to his parents, sharing his heart's desire to reach others with the Gospel. "Sometimes when we feel like we are losing control, it brings us face to face with the fact that we aren't the ones who are in charge, God is. If we give our lives to Him and even if we die for Him, we aren't going to tell Jesus, 'See, I knew it wouldn't work!' If to live is Christ and to die is gain, then I guess we just can't lose."

After graduating from the Institute, Jay prepared for missionary service by starting as a pre-seminary major at Cedarville College. Challenged by the need to reach the unsaved in his college town, Jay did not wait until finishing seminary to have a ministry. For two years Jay witnessed door-to-door until he had been to every home in the town. After attending a Christmas missionary conference with his fiancé in 1985, Jay rededicated his life to the Lord and returned to school the next month with an even greater desire to make his life count for God. He shared his concern for the lost with a friend one day as he remarked, "I would be willing to give my life if others (Christians) would be challenged to get right with God and begin serving Him."

Just a few days later, on February 18, 1986, Jay was involved in an automobile accident, and God called him Home. In a letter to Jack Wyrtzen a few days after their son's death, the Butchers wrote, "We know that as much as God was using Jay to influence those around him while he was living, He never would have taken Jay Home had He not intended to use Jay's life and testimony to have an even greater impact through his death. How we praise God that Jay learned to serve Him now, not years from now."

Many homes have a guest room where visitors can be sheltered and ministered to before going on their way once again. In the Word of Life Bible Institute, Christian young people have a place where they are ministered to and cared for, where they are challenged to make right their spiritual shortcomings, and where they are equipped for going out into the world to serve the Lord. Jack Wyrtzen said the three stages of the Christian life are to know, to grow, and to show – and through the

Word of Life Bible Institute, Jack's vision will have an impact for God only eternity will reveal, as young people train and prepare to become the dynamic Christian leaders of tomorrow.

CHAPTER 12

The Plumbing

...admonishing one another in psalms and hymns and spiritual songs... Colossians 3:16

One by one, the students from Nyack Missionary College were introduced to share their testimonies. As he listened to each speaker address the conference near his home in downtown New York City, Tony Bollback was thrilled by the many exciting stories he heard from mission fields around the world. "That's what I should have done with my life instead of throwing it away," Tony thought to himself, "but now I've missed it!" That night at the missions conference, Tony made a promise to the Lord – a promise that the Lord could have his three children to work full time for Him. God held Tony to that promise, as a few years later his first son left for missionary work in China. When his second son, Harry, left in 1950 to evangelize the Indians in Brazil, the elder Bollback thought about the ministry his son was leaving as staff pianist for evangelist, Jack Wyrtzen. Tony wondered, "Will my son ever use his musical gifts again?"

Indeed, influenced by the vision and encouragement of Jack Wyrtzen, Harry Bollback was set aside for many years as God's man to start the Word of Life overseas ministries – first in Brazil with his colleague, Harold Reimer, and then around the world. During those exciting years, Harry wrote many stirring songs of commitment such as "I Will Go" and "Not My Will," which are still enjoyed today. But, during that time of his life, Harry accepted as his chief calling God's clear leading into missions. However, God's Word tells us in Ecclesiastes 3:1: *To everything there is a season, a time for every purpose under heaven.* By the mid-1970's, the Word of Life overseas ministries had become firmly established on all six inhabited continents, so that the work was now being carried on by scores of able, dedicated Christians.

The Lord, therefore, laid a new desire on Harry's heart, a desire he shared with Jack for reaching young people with the Gospel of Christ in a dynamic, new way suited to today's generation. While still a missionary in Brazil, Harry wrote a musical play entitled "Not My Will," depicting his experiences among the jungle Indians. Over the years, he saw the production translated and produced in other lands. "Why don't you write some more music?" Jack asked. But Harry had never tried anything on such a large scale as Jack suggested – scores, sets, costumes, staging, and lighting. Without any professional experience, how could he do it? But Jack persisted, and, in 1976, Harry produced the musical, "Let Freedom Ring."

Jack Wyrtzen believed God had brought together all the elements for a unique and fruitful music ministry that would not have been possible in the earlier years of the organization. Young people brought up on television might not sit through an old-style mass rally but could be attracted to a powerful and highly visual presentation of Gospel truths. Electronic technology had developed so much that impressive multi- media productions were possible at a reasonable cost. The Word of Life Bible Institute at Schroon Lake was then in its sixth year and had grown to several hundred students, so all the performers and stage help needed to conduct a successful concert tour were right at hand. And finally, God had brought in Harry Bollback, the right man to put the details together.

Thus, America's bicentennial year is also an important year in the history of Word of Life. In 1976, Harry Bollback and the first group of Word of Life Collegians left Schroon Lake for the very first Word of Life tour. With a group of 50 singers, the presentation of "Let Freedom Ring" so impressed the public, that it was later produced by Word of Life as a nationwide television special.

For many years following, the Collegians crisscrossed the country in air-conditioned motor coaches, presenting several tours each year that lasted from two weeks to two months. Using state-of-the-art stage technology, Word of Life produced other original Bollback musical dramas such as "Ring the Bells, "His Truth Goes Marching On," "America, We Still Believe in You," "God, Country and Decency," "The Passion Play," "God's Portrait of Love," "The Sights and Sounds of Christmas," "America, I Still Can Hear Your Song," "The Revelation," "Daniel," and "Genesis." Through the years, more than two million people in 1,500 cities across America – and in Canada and the British Isles – attended Word of Life concerts.

However, far more important is the harvest of souls the Lord allowed through this unique and dynamic outreach. Beginning with the first tour in 1976, more than 100,000 persons accepted the invitation to receive Jesus as their own Savior – and thousands more rededicated their lives to God. People who might never have attended a church service or an evangelistic meeting came to see and hear Gospel truths presented in an entertaining, yet powerful way.

"I went to see 'The Passion Play,' when you came to our area," wrote one attendee, "and the dramatization was terrific. I could not hold back the tears during the crucifixion scene. It really touched my heart, and words cannot express the impact it had on my life. Please pray for my sister and her boyfriend who went forward to accept Christ at the end of the program. Praise the Lord! God is certainly good, isn't He?"

Then another attendee who saw "The Revelation" wrote, "It all started when the scene of the Lake of Fire came on. I had a feeling inside that the Lord loved me. Tears of happiness filled my eyes as I accepted Jesus into my heart."

Every tour brought special stories of people whose hearts were touched by the Spirit of God while seeing a Word of Life musical drama. One incident, still very much remembered, happened at an October

presentation of "The Revelation" in Phoenix, Arizona. A young lady came up after the concert to share her testimony:

"Five years ago, I attended the Word of Life 'Revelation' concert for the first time. When the invitation was given, I did not go forward with the others, but there in my seat I knew I had to do something about my relationship to Christ. I was a rebellious 17-year-old whose actions were destroying my parents. I left that night to go to the apartment of the man with whom I was living. I packed my bags and went home to my parents, and, that night, the Lord saved me." Through the ministry of Word of Life's presentation, God reached down and performed spiritual surgery on her rebellious heart. As everyone listened, she turned and introduced her husband of 18 months. "We're planning on coming to the Word of Life Bible Institute next September."

Much of Word of Life's ministry is youth-oriented, as church polls reveal that 85 percent of Christians make salvation decisions before age 21. The probability of making a decision for Christ gets progressively lower as one gets older, until only 1 in every 750,000 people over age 75 will accept an invitation to receive Christ as Savior. Yet, through this unique ministry, 30 percent of those who came forward were over 60 years of age, and many of these are even in their 80's!

Harry Bollback is especially fond of recalling one unforgettable night after a concert in Poughkeepsie, New York. When the invitation was given, an elderly gentleman slipped from his place to come to the front. Meanwhile, the lady seated beside him remained with her head bowed in prayer. When the invitation was finished, this lady bolted down the aisle in tears to embrace her husband. She had been praying for him for 35 years!

All the musical dramas presented by Word of Life were produced entirely in-house – with a powerful dose of help from the Lord. The logistics of staging a half dozen concert tours each year, seen by 200,000 people in some 175 cities, was a mammoth undertaking. Performers, drama coaches, engineers, photographers, drivers, set builders, costume designers – all were Word of Life students or staff.

First, of course, each play had to be written and its music arranged and scored. Next, the staging, costuming, set designs, and lighting and sound engineering were meticulously worked out. Multi-image audio-visual presentations enhanced most Word of Life productions, using up to 18 projectors and thousands of slides, which were synchronized by a computer. Performers were selected from Word of Life students, and travel occurred during semester breaks or after graduation. Lines and songs were memorized, acting scenes rehearsed, costume fittings, and makeup applied. Meanwhile, the dedicated staff in the Word of Life Tour Department was constantly on the telephone setting itineraries, printing tickets and posters, and arranging for auditoriums, meals, and housing. In addition, even the motor coaches and an eighteen-wheel trailer needed to transport crew and equipment across the country were all owned and maintained by Word of Life.

Yet, when it all came together, audiences were treated to such powerful and moving scenes as The Crucifixion, The Empty Tomb, and The Glory of Jesus from "The Passion Play" ...or The Great Tribulation, The Great White Throne, The Lake of Fire and The New Jerusalem from "The Revelation," ...or The Creation, Noah and the Ark, Sodom and Gomorrah, and The Mount of Transfiguration from "Genesis."

Word of Life musical groups gave presentations before capacity crowds at such places as Madison Square Garden, Philadelphia Civic Center, Constitution Hall, Washington Convention Center, Disneyland, and Disney World.

Those on the road spent up to two months on tour, performing each night in a different city and then spreading out for a good night's rest in different area homes, before the next day's travel. The full impact of this ministry will only be known in eternity, but many reports were received each year such as the following:

During an autumn tour, the hall was packed in Concord, New Hampshire, for a Friday night presentation of the "Daniel" concert. At the invitation, a 17-year-old boy came down from the balcony to be saved. The following Sunday, the pastor called to say this young man had been in a car accident and was with the Lord.

While presenting the spring tour in Toms River, New Jersey, an 82-year-old lady responded to the invitation to accept Christ as her Savior. A few days later, a local pastor looked over the decision slips and decided he would visit this lady. As he approached her home, he saw a rescue squad van parked in front. The woman had suffered a heart attack and within minutes had gone Home to be with the Lord.

A young lady had made a decision for salvation through Christ at a Word of Life winter tour in Florida. The following week she was found murdered in her home.

"When your earth-life was ready to begin," intones the narration of "The Passion Play", "before you had even seen the light of this world, God reached out and touched the pendulum of your heart, and it began its millions of beats. Someday His finger will reach out and touch your heart again, and its beatings will be over. When? We know not. You need not care, if you know Christ. ...to live is Christ, and to die is gain."

In 1998, a transition took place in this ministry, and Word of Life Tours continued on under the new name, Gospel Productions, in a permanent venue at the Harry Bollback Performing Arts Center in Hudson, Florida. Harry's ministry continued as his original programs, "The Sights and Sounds of Christmas" and "The Passion Play", were adapted and presented to almost 200,000 people at that location. Of more importance are the thousands of lives who came to Christ through these dynamic programs.

Just as the plumbing carries cleansing, life-giving water to every part of the house, so Word of Life musical drama presentations brought the Living Water of God's Word throughout North America and in many countries around the world. The inception of this ministry and indeed the phenomenal growth of Word of Life over the years is also a tribute to Jack Wyrtzen's ability to share the leadership. Vision has always been a characteristic of Jack, and he transmitted that dynamic trait to Harry Bollback as well. Word of Life began with the conversion and dream of Jack Wyrtzen but multiplied as Jack allowed others to use their gifts to serve the Lord.

CHAPTER 13

The Study

Holding fast the faithful word...
Titus 1:9

It was Monday morning after a long weekend of meetings. Jack looked through his correspondence and found on his desk this letter from Venezuela:

Dear Jack,

Just got back here to the Venezuelan border after these last six months of conferences. Was glad to receive your letter and to know that the letter I sent back in January had actually arrived. The Indian fellow was supposed to go to San Fernando with my mail within a few days of the January conference. However, he stopped on the way down to work for some people. You know how they figure, 'What difference does three or four months make?' I also received a Christmas photo of you and Marge and all. A real cute-looking tribe, I must say. The Indians just love to look at the picture.

They are especially interested because it was through you and Marge that they are not in their drunken witchcraft ceremonies on the road to Hell anymore, but on their way to Heaven instead. At the conference this year we baptized about one hundred and fifty Indians – only adults. There are many witch doctors and others to be reached with the Gospel. Glad to hear that the Lord is blessing more than ever in your meet-

ings there in the States. Thanks again, Jack, for everything; but most of all I thank you and Marge for getting me started on this. Every time I stop to think of what it means to be in our kind of work, I can't help but say, 'What an amazing undeserved privilege to be accepted as a co-laborer of the Almighty Creator.'

Yours in Christ, Sophie

Yes, that is what makes it all worthwhile. One day as Jack was talking to the Council members of Word of Life, he reminded them that it wasn't how many buildings they had or how many acres of land or how many radio and TV stations they were on or even how many camps they had around the world. What really counts is that people's lives are changed and that they go on to do something for the Lord.

Jack pushed his chair back from his desk and thought about Sophie. At that very moment she was trekking through the jungles of South America reaching Indians with the Gospel. Way back in the early days of Word of Life, Sophie Muller had been to a street meeting where Jack and Marge were giving their testimonies. She was surprised to hear Jack stand up and talk about the Lord, and then she couldn't believe her ears when she heard Marge say that she had been saved. So, she stayed around to find out more about it. As she talked with Jack and Marge, the Lord began to speak to Sophie's heart in a very real way. Before long, Sophie received the Lord into her heart; she was saved.

Now, what was she going to do with her life? She was already a commercial artist doing work for some of the popular magazines in America. Her life was made. Even though she was young, she was on her way up.

Then she heard about the mission field. She left her career plans behind, and after Bible school she went to the jungles, a woman alone, going to places where no civilized person had ever been before. She invented systems of teaching the Indians how to read and write in a very short period of time. Sometimes she just disappeared in the jungle – a year or two at a time. No one knew if she was alive or even where she was. She just lived with the people.

Jack remembered the day when Sophie Muller was home on furlough and he asked her; "Sophie, how many believers do you have out there now? How many have been baptized? How many churches do you have?"

Sophie thought for a moment, and she said, "Jack, at this time, as far as I know, there are two hundred and forty churches now established with about twelve thousand believers."

Results: This is what gives Word of Life meaning. Before Sophie went Home to Heaven, she had led thousands more to the Lord. Today, a Bible Institute has been started to train believers in the work of the Lord. These are among the many dividends from the dollars that God's people have invested to help Word of Life reach needy people with the life-changing message of the Gospel.

Jack picked up another letter:

Dear Jack,

I've been praying for you almost every day. Praise the Lord for the fantastic way He has been using you. I'll forever thank the Lord for the wonderful day at Word of Life Island when I came to know the Lord Jesus Christ as my Savior. May the Lord continue to bless you. ~ Keita

Jack remembered Keita very well. He was a Japanese university student who a few years before had come to Word of Life Island. Keita had thought that Christianity was an American and European religion and that Buddhism and Shintoism were best for Orientals. Jack had just featured Keita's testimony on a Word of Life radio program, and he remembered Keita saying that during his second summer in America he was working at a hospital in Glenn City, Pennsylvania. In that hospital there was a nurse who was constantly witnessing to him; she had told him about Christ many times. He wasn't interested in Christianity at all, but he pretended he was, because he didn't want to disappoint this young lady. Every time she gave him some Christian literature, he would accept it and stick it in his pocket. He had to be polite because that's what Americans always thought of Orientals, and he didn't want to ruin the image.

As soon as he got home, he threw everything in the wastebasket. One day she told him that there was a fantastic vacation place called Word of Life. She had already contacted the people there and found out that he could spend a week there on a scholarship. She talked to Keita's boss and got permission for him to take a week off from work. She was a very kind person and made every arrangement for this trip. He just didn't understand why she was so excited about his vacation.

He soon arrived at Word of Life Island. When Jack gave the invitation, after explaining that Jesus Christ is God's Son who came to die for our sins, Keita said that for the first time in his life he understood the Lord Jesus Christ had died on the cross for his sins. When he heard that Jesus Christ loved him enough to die for him, he just couldn't reject Him. At the end of the first meeting, he trusted the Lord Jesus Christ as his own personal Savior.

His counselor helped him throughout the week. He spent time every day in the Word. It was step by step. Four days after his conversion he was out witnessing to others. Jack remembered how he suggested to Keita that he write his family in Japan about his decision. He remembered so well Keita's keen disappointment when his family wrote back and told how upset they were that he had become a Christian and that he was going to be involved in the ministry.

But as soon as Keita finished college, he went back to Japan and had the opportunity to lead his mother, his father, and many of his family

and close relatives to Jesus Christ.

Results: This is what makes it all worthwhile. Jack continued reading the letters on his desk.

Dear Jack,

Last summer I was on Word of Life Island, and I got converted. I am *fifteen years old, and I have a job after school. I would like to send the enclosed $20 to Word of Life so I can be a great help in getting other kids to Christ. I am looking forward to coming again next year to camp.*

~ Neil

Another letter from Medina, Ohio, said:

Your program on the radio played a large part in my decision to accept Christ as my personal Savior. Thank you so much. I listen while milking my cows. ~ Don

The next letter was from Nevada:

Dear Jack,

The enclosed $1 carries a story of the joy that was ours just a few days ago. Our little boy, Mark, is just a few months under six years. The other night at our evening devotional time we read your prayer letter concerning the need in Brazil. Usually he doesn't seem to pay very close attention, but this time I noticed he was very quiet and had a sort of a 'faraway look' in his eyes. Your letter mentioned the amount of $200,000 for the Bible Institute buildings in Brazil. When we had finished reading the Word and praying for your work in Brazil, little Mark went to check his bank – an old cigar box! He wanted to send you a dollar, but he had only sixty cents. To shorten the story, he did all sorts of extra work, even scrubbing floors, in order to get his sixty cents up to a dollar. And so here it is, sent by a little boy with a heart that was touched by his Savior. He has professed receiving the Lord Jesus for a year now, and it is evidence such as this that gives us a cause of praise. Needless to say, his bank is depleted, but his little cup (and ours) is running over. May our lovely Lord Jesus take this dollar and use it to make the difference in winning Brazil to Himself.

In our Savior's love, John

From Lewiston, Pennsylvania, one young lady wrote:

I just wanted to send a little note along telling everyone at Word of Life *camp that the one week I spent with you changed my whole life. Accepting Christ into my heart made me the happiest person alive. I consider it a privilege to send $5 a month to help support such a worthy cause.*

Love in Jesus, Lisa

A high school student wrote:

I won the enclosed $15 in a high school speaking contest. I was speaking to the juniors and seniors, and I presented the salvation message to 900 students who attended. ~ David

The next letter was from New Jersey:

Do you remember me? I'm David. Remember when my girlfriend got saved and dedicated her life; well, she really inspired me to work better for the Lord. So, guess what?! I led two of my friends to Christ today. It was really marvelous. I led my friend, Robert, to the Lord on the steps of our old hangout. First, I asked him if he knew where he was going after he died, and he admitted he was going to Hell. Then I told him I was going to Heaven. He asked me how I knew. Then I showed him from the Bible. After he read it, he was so amazed; he said he never heard of anything so great. He asked and begged me to tell him more. So, I told him how I was saved, and how once you're saved, you're always His, and how He is building a place for us in Heaven, and how to grow with the Lord. Then we took a walk and talked some more. Robert had the biggest smile on his face I have ever seen. His first words to me were, 'David, I'm going to Heaven.' Let me tell you, I never felt so happy! He prayed out loud, and he accepted the Lord Jesus into his heart. I'm so excited; I'm having trouble writing this letter! He couldn't believe how happy he felt, and he wanted to tell everybody about Jesus Christ, so we found two of our friends, Mark and Steve, and we led Steve to Christ. He was all in tears. I still can't believe it. And we got Mark to think about Jesus Christ and salvation. We're going to start a Word of Life Club of our own; Robert is so anxious to learn about God. All I can say is that I wish I knew more to tell him. I wrote this letter 'cause I thought you'd be happy about it. And I want you to write back and tell me what you think and give me some more enthusiasm and Scriptures.

God bless you, David

Every day, hundreds of letters came in from all over the United States and the world through radio programs heard on many stations here in America and overseas. Jack once said, "I would like to take off a week just to praise the Lord when I think of His great victories, but there are too many new battles to be won."

Victories don't come easy – there's always a price to pay. Jack knew that if he was to be effective, there must be discipline. He had to discipline himself. Right from the very beginning the Bible became the textbook of his life. He studied it. And as he studied, he became convinced that his message was not to explain the miracles, or even the inspiration of the Bible, but his message was that of, 'Thus saith the Lord.'

Reading and studying the Bible was as natural to Jack as breathing. His breakfast was usually orange juice, coffee, and the Bible. He spent hours every day reading. His thirst for the knowledge of the Word of God was unquenchable.

In the days right after Jack's salvation, he traveled on the New York City subway to and from his business. This gave him about two hours of time for studying the Word of God every day. Almost everybody on the subway read the newspaper. Usually, people were so jammed in that all they could do was rest their papers on some other passenger's back. Even if you didn't have your own paper, you could read over somebody's shoulder. Instead of reading the newspaper, Jack read the "Good News" – the Bible – every day and held it high enough so that others could read it over his shoulder.

Jack stood for the defense of the faith and the proclamation of the Gospel. To Jack, things were right or wrong –black or white – people were saved or lost. There was no middle ground – no gray areas. Jack never compromised on his Biblical position regardless of what it might cost him personally. People loved him because of his position.

A singing celebrity named Tiny Tim, famous for his long hair and feminine voice, contacted Jack. Often, he would call and talk to Jack by the hour. Because of this friendship, Tiny Tim asked Jack to perform his wedding ceremony on national television during the Johnny Carson "Tonight" show. Jack assured Tiny Tim that he would be glad to do so if he would do the following things:

1. Join a church
2. Get baptized
3. Cut his hair
4. Quit show business
5. Go to Bible school for one year

Tiny Tim had made some sort of a decision with Jack; however, Jack believed, if any man be in Christ, he is a new creation.

Tiny Tim wouldn't make the break. He felt he couldn't follow Jack's requirements. The ceremony took place on the TV talk show but not with Jack Wyrtzen.

A full-time staff member who had just made some musical recordings for Word of Life was caught in sin. His record albums had arrived that very day at camp. Not only was the man dismissed within the hour, but the next day all the recordings were disposed of as well.

When a famous evangelist came to New York for his second crusade in 1969, Jack found it impossible to cooperate as he had in the first New York crusade. The evangelist had instituted an all-inclusive policy of handing over decision slips for follow up to liberal churches, according to the converts' denominational preferences. Though Jack prayed regularly for that evangelist and thanked God for all those saved through the crusades, his stand cost him many friends. Jack's principles and convictions were based on God's Word and were consistent. He could not ignore his heart's dictates. He said, "I would preach at the Vatican if they would invite me." And he would have done it. Jack said, "I'll preach on their platform anytime, but they don't preach on mine." Sometimes that got him into difficult situations.

In the Midwest, a rally was planned by some Christian businessmen. In their interest to get many people to the meeting, they secured the cooperation of many churches and groups. All this was unknown to Jack Wyrtzen. When he arrived and saw the situation, he refused to take an offering. He told the committee that he didn't want money for the Lord's work from a group of that type. He preached and gave an invitation; the response was overwhelming. When Jack preached a message, he didn't speak in generalities. He hit hard; he fought sin. Some of his favorite targets were rock music, provocative dress, drugs, alcohol, homosexuality, and sexual immorality.

Jack was very sincere about money. Some years ago, a man gave Jack a check for $10,000. The ministry needed it desperately. While Jack was chatting with the man, he discovered that the man was not a believer but thought that he was buying his way to Heaven by giving this gift to Word of Life. Jack graciously refused the check and told the man why.

Honor thy father and thy mother, was more than just a phrase in the Bible to Jack. He welcomed his elderly father-in-law into his home and personally took care of him until his death. Years later both of Jack's parents needed personal care, and he willingly opened the doors of his home to these aging loved ones.

The following letter from three young people, who were "hippies" before their conversion, shows the deep love and special interest Jack had for people.

Dear Jack,

Tom, Harry and I want to thank you from the bottom of our hearts for letting us be your guests at camp. We had more enjoyment being with other Christians than can be imagined. We thank you for being a father to us. We love and respect you and know that truly your life is dedicated for the Lord's service. Often when I look at you, I don't see you, but Christ. Your testimony and vision and warm heart toward us has continually encouraged and blessed us. P.S. We got to witness to the whole

Greyhound Bus crew coming home. We love you very much.

There are people all over the world who felt this way about Jack. In Korea, he met a young soldier who had been saved at Word of Life camp just before he was shipped overseas. He said, "I just couldn't understand you. Why should you take so much interest in me?"

Even before he was saved, Jack had great concern for people. When he was just twelve years old, he was awarded the Boy Scout Medal of Honor for saving an entire family. Having arrived at a fellow scout's home to coach him for his tenderfoot test, Jack found the family overcome by gas. His fast action made the difference. He notified the police, opened the windows, and gave first aid, reviving and rescuing all the members of the family.

In the early days through the influence of a Chinese evangelist, Jack was introduced to the N.B.N.P.N.B. Club. That meant No Bible, No Prayer – No Breakfast. It was when Jack meditated and studied the Word that the principles of his life were established.

Right from the very beginning he had to decide if he was going to be popular or stand true to the Word of God. While many others compromised and sold out for a few dollars and perhaps fame, Jack stood his ground – many times alone. Some liberals hated him – he's too dogmatic, over-simplified, and too fundamental. Some fundamentalists said he was not separated enough. But some evangelists said he was too separated and, therefore, unaware of the issues.

The issue Jack saw was that men without Christ are lost in sin and need a Savior. But that didn't mean that everything else was forgotten in preference to the Gospel or that Jack would cooperate with all groups and churches just so he could preach to more people.

In a message, Jack said:

There is more and more pressure on us from outside sources to leave the good old paths and ancient landmarks. I want you to know that as far as Word of Life is concerned, we are alarmed over the recent pub-

lic announcements that have been coming from the World Council of Churches, from the National Council of Churches, and from many of the local Protestant Council of Churches. As Protestants we bow our heads in shame.

I want you to know that as far as Word of Life is concerned, we are not in any way associated with the World Council of Churches, the National Council of Churches, nor any Protestant Council of Churches who are connected with the Ecumenical Movement. We stand only with the evangelical Christians around the world who believe the Bible to be the inerrant, infallible, verbally inspired Word of God. And we will continue by the grace of God, as He gives us the strength, to preach the old-fashioned Gospel of Jesus Christ, how Christ died for our sins and is now risen from the grave for our justification.

CHAPTER 14

The Roof

...your Shepherd, the Guardian of your souls, Who keeps you safe from all attacks. 1 Peter 2:25 – The Living New Testament

Through the years of building this house, God has blessed in a remarkable way. The Master Architect has put it all together for His honor and glory. He knows each room, the people in them, and has seen fit to cover it all with His blessing. The roof of this house has drawn together all the rooms. It has guarded its occupants from the attacks of their enemies. It has been like an umbrella of God's protection over the entire construction.

Actually, many things that took place and are taking place today were never really planned by Jack. It is God's house. He is not only the Architect, but the Builder. This is why Jack loved to sing, "To God Be the Glory, Great Things He Hath Done." He chose that hymn many times for his meetings. Another one of his favorites and one he sang heartily was "I'm a Child of the King," and as a child of the King, he knew "He owns the cattle on a thousand hills, the wealth in every mine." He knew that... No good thing will He withhold from them that walk uprightly. Jack walked by faith, believing God.

In all reality, this house did not just happen. God used a man – a man who was available, who truly, sincerely and with all his might loved and trusted Him, and a man with explicit and almost childlike faith that God would do the impossible.

Time has changed some things, yet the blessing continues.

As Jack looked out and saw the desperate need of men to know God and His Son, Jesus Christ, to have their sins forgiven, to live lives pleasing to Him because one day the Return of the Lord was coming, he rapidly became an evangelist reaching the masses with the Gospel. In the 1940's and 50's there wasn't an auditorium in the East that didn't fill to capacity with overflowing crowds to hear the message of salvation through Jesus Christ preached by Jack Wyrtzen. Seven different times Madison Square Garden couldn't contain the crowds in New York. Once on a rainy day in 1948, more than 40,000 attended the great Word of Life rally in Yankee Stadium, and some 1,200 people made decisions for Christ that day.

Jack was then known the world over as perhaps the greatest evangelist to youth. The radio ministry was expanding. Then in 1949 Word of Life went coast-to-coast on TV with an exciting program reaching youth and families alike with the Gospel. But things changed.

In 1946 when the Island in Schroon Lake was purchased, a new ministry began. Jack became a camp director, a youth speaker, and an expert with teenagers. The Word of Life ministry grew to encircle the world. Camps have been established on six continents with plans for as many as the Lord allows. Word of Life Bible Clubs, now called Local Church Ministries, continue to increase in number and impact in local churches across the United States, Canada and overseas.

In 1970 when the Word of Life Bible Institute opened, things began to change again, and as time goes on and the Lord delays His coming, things will continue to change. New rooms will be added. This is a healthy sign. What a few years ago was a one-man ministry has developed today, under God, into a large force of people all committed to the same task – that of reaching people with the Good News that Jesus saves; He forgives sin; He changes lives, and He is coming again to receive His own unto Himself. All that has taken place in Word of Life is because Jack Wyrtzen was willing to pay the price and to be God's man.

Connected closely with Jack throughout his ministry was the Word of Life Council, which was a large group of committed people who sincerely loved the Lord and who personally believed in what Jack was doing under God. These close friends gave Jack, through their counsel and prayers, the support he needed to continue the job. Jack constantly looked to this group for help. Proverbs 11:14 teaches that... *In the multitude of counselors there is safety.*

Some things have changed very little over the years. One is the Board of Directors. New members have been added as God has called some Home to be with Him, but the Board remains as a group who love and are dedicated to the ministry of Word of Life. The solidness of the ministry today and its stability can easily be traced back to Jack's great ability to bring and to keep together this group.

Another thing that has never changed is the message – the strong Biblical position, not only in doctrine, but Christian standards of conduct. Jack's great love for people stayed strong from the time God first gave him the vision and compassion for men lost and degraded in their sin and unbelief. Individuals were never lost in the crowd. His ability to see people, not as they were but as they could be in Jesus Christ, was a great part of his personality. He had a sincere love and concern for his friends and for the staff.

Jack loved the Word of God, and this love constantly grew as he saturated himself in it. His faith was in an unchanging God with unchanging standards. Jack said, "I believe it took more faith to trust God back in the old days for a few dollars than it does today for thousands."

After being on the radio for just a short time, Jack began to receive invitations to go and preach in many places. His original crowd of friends and other Christian young people whom he had met had gone on to different schools across the country. He had met many different pastors and laymen, and they had all told him, "When you are in our area, be sure you drop in and see us. Stay with us."

Shortly after Jack had given up his job in the insurance company to go full time preaching the Word, he and Marge took a trip to Chicago. They had been invited by one of the students at Moody Bible Institute to speak at the chapel. They were prepared to preach in different places on the trip out and back. As they left New York, they headed for Albany with $15 in their pocket. "Here in Albany," Jack said, "Christian friends put us up for the night, fed us and gave us five or six dollars, so that after paying for gas and other expenses, we still had about $15, so we headed on to Buffalo."

Previously they had met a friend who had told them he would set up a week of meetings in the Buffalo area. Jack wrote, and even though his friend never wrote back, he just assumed that everything was moving ahead. By the time they arrived in Niagara Falls they were down to $9. They telephoned their friend only to find out that a meeting was planned for Sunday, and this was only Tuesday. They were told to find a nice place to stay, enjoy themselves and "everything was all set for Sunday." Their $9 was hardly enough for room and board anyplace for six days! Jack said, "We looked at Niagara Falls from every angle that was free; then we would sleep late in the morning so we wouldn't be hungry for breakfast, and then we'd buy some rolls or buns in a bakery for lunch." The rooming house where they stayed was beyond description. In fact, Jack tied the bed together with a rope to keep it from falling apart. Somehow the money lasted until Sunday, and then they were broke!

When the meetings were over on Sunday night, they handed Jack a check. Outside the church he looked at it, $10! As he and Marge got into the old Chevy to head towards Chicago, they said to each other, "Guess they thought we were rich radio preachers from New York."

As they drove on toward Chicago, in the back of Jack's mind was the thought that certainly the great Moody Bible Institute would take good care of them. However, once again when they arrived, no one really knew they were coming, since it had only been the suggestion of one of the students. The students put them up in a cheap rundown hotel across from the school. It wasn't the greatest, by far, but they

were there, and it was a place to stay. The meetings they had were the devotional periods in the students' dorms.

God knows the reasons for His actions and the purpose behind the experiences He allows his servants to go through. He was building a structure and was testing the foundation to make sure it was strong.

It was at this time, while they were in Chicago, that they met Harry Saulnier, director of the famous Pacific Garden Mission. He prayed with the young inexperienced evangelist, gave him some good books by William R. Newell, along with some good techniques for street meeting work. He also called on Jack and Marge to give testimonies at the mission. At the end of the week, someone slipped them a dollar or two or three.

Heading back to New York, the young couple, so anxious to serve the Lord with everything they had, stopped in Cleveland. Several people came to know the Lord in the meeting they had there. Jack says, "I believe it was April 1, and I was going to try out a new sermon for April Fool's Day, preaching on five kinds of fools in the Bible. I preached and some got saved."

Mr. And Mrs. Bruce Musselman, directors of the Union Gospel Press, took Jack and Marge to their home when the meeting was over. Somehow this man sensed this young couple was exhausted and suggested they sleep in the next morning. About 10:00 a.m. they had a good meal with the Musselmans before leaving for Binghamton, New York. As they were leaving, they had prayer together, and Mr. Musselman slipped Jack a five- dollar bill. They got in the car to leave, and as Jack turned the ignition key, his eye caught the gas gauge, and it read "full." Mr. Musselman had filled the tank. He rushed out of the car to thank him, and as he returned, his eyes fell toward the tires – four new tires had been put on his car as he and Marge had slept! How good God was. He had met every need.

When they arrived in Binghamton, they had about $18. The meeting there was in a little country church outside the city, and Jack and Marge were welcomed into the pastor's home for the night. It was easy to see that this little preacher and his wife were not in the ministry for what they could get out of it. They were poor. They had real financial needs themselves, and the pastor was still a student. Somehow the Wyrtzens found out they didn't even have money that was due for their rent the next day. Jack said they had a pretty good crowd out for a little country church. The pastor stood up and made a real financial appeal for Word of Life. Jack recalled, "I think they gave about $6, plus a few buttons and some other things in the offering." That night as the minister was closing up the church, Marge turned to Jack and said, "You are not going to keep that offering, are you? He needs it more than we do." Jack remembers he was still a little hesitant to give him the money. They still had to get back to New York. They would be returning with just about the same amount they left with. No money for the work, and really not too much to tell the gang about. Jack was concerned. Should they give the offering to the young minister or take it for Word of Life? He said, "I figured that Marge had the right leading, so we handed the fellow the bag with the offering in it and said, 'You keep it.'" He insisted that Jack take it. Jack continued, "We thanked him for it, and told him he had given it to us, but we felt the Lord wanted us to give it back to him. He took the money, and I remember he broke down and cried. Finally, he said, 'You know, I have my car parked over there on the top of the hill without any gas. You didn't know it, but my rent was due tomorrow morning, and the landlord told me that if we didn't pay it tomorrow morning, we were going to have to get out.' His rent was $4, so with the $6 he paid for his rent and gasoline."

That was the pioneer evangelistic tour for Jack and Marge Wyrtzen and the Word of Life ministry. They had traveled about 18 days, returned with the same amount of money they had started with, but many people had found Christ as Savior. And all their physical needs were met.

In 1990, almost 50 years to the day after that first Word of Life speaking tour, Jack was in Hudson, Florida, to cut the ribbon and welcome the first guests to Word of Life's new Conference Center and Youth Camp.

The Conference Center is located in one of the fastest-growing sections of the southeast, just 30 miles north of Tampa on 500 acres of prime real estate donated to Word of Life in 1985. By 1990, this undeveloped tract of land was transformed into a beautiful adult Conference Center and a spectacular Youth Camp. Other facilities include the 1200-seat Harry Bollback Performing Arts Center – home of Word of Life's Gospel Productions, a spacious dining room, a bookstore, tennis courts, and a beautifully-heated pool.

A companion to the Conference Center is a spectacular Youth Camp, all in a setting the Lord is using to draw hundreds of youth to Himself in salvation and dedication. Among the towering pine and oak trees are individual cabins, a large auditorium and dining hall, and basketball, tennis, and volleyball courts. There was all this plus a trained and caring staff to provide the same Christ-centered program that has made Word of Life distinctive in its worldwide camping ministries. Through God's blessing, this facility has become the spiritual birthplace for thousands of young people.

Far from slowing down, Word of Life was actually picking up speed as it continued into its second half-century of Christ-centered ministry. Through careful planning, Jack and the present leadership sought God's guidance in training a new generation of leaders so that the ministry would not stagnate with years but would grow and move ahead in reaching out to people with the Gospel of Christ through new and expanding ministries.

Jack would have considered himself a failure if Word of Life wasn't prepared to continue without him, and so he prepared for the day when leadership of the ministry would pass on to other men. The need to plan for an orderly and effective transition of leadership hit home in 1981 when Jack and Harry Bollback were planning a tour of Korea. The two would be traveling extensively within the country by helicopter, and Jack remarked, "You know, Harry, we should tell the Board of Directors who we'd choose as our successor if we were killed. Why don't you write your choice on a piece of paper?" Harry wrote his selection and then showed it to Jack. It was the same name Jack had in mind! – George Theis, the Director of Word of Life camps in Recife, Brazil. Two years later, George rejoined the home staff as Co-Director, beginning the process of assuring stable and dynamic leadership for the future.

Through more than 50 years of ministry, without reservation, Jack chose to stand with Joshua of old to fear the Lord, to serve Him in sincerity and truth. Old things, old desires for self were put aside, and Jack stood firm as he preached out the message found in Joshua 24:15: Choose you this day whom you will serve... as for me and my house, we will serve the Lord.

Jack Wyrtzen was greatly used of God not only for his ability but also for his availability. As the Great Architect was drawing up His plans for this building, He looked for a man, one to whom He could trust His work, and He found one.

CHAPTER 15

PHASE I: Construction Completed!

Precious in the sight of the Lord is the death of his saints.
Psalm 116:15

On April 20, 1996, Jack Wyrtzen's body was laid to rest in Schroon Lake, New York, awaiting the Return of the Lord for His Church. When a loved one goes to be with the Lord, someone has to go through all the papers, letters, photos and memorabilia to separate what is important and what should be thrown away. There was much to sort through concerning Jack. His life had touched so many people, not only his wife and immediate family, but a much larger family all over the world. As the material was collected and correlated, there were many things that came into focus. Many friends and fellow workers confirmed what had been found in the archives as they expressed what Jack Wyrtzen had meant to them and had contributed to the work of the Lord.

Jack will always be vibrant and very much alive in my memory and in the hearts and memories of multitudes of others. He truly was a great man, and it was a privilege to have worked with him and to have been his friend. He is greatly missed. I was sixteen, and a senior in high school in New York. Then one day someone got word to my parents that Jack Wyrtzen would like to hear me play my trumpet... our friendship was launched. The greatest impact Jack had on my life was spiritual. Here was a man who was completely sold out to the Lord, and anyone on his team was expected to be the same. At one of the Saturday Night Rallies in New York, he met a young Navy lieutenant by the name of Clyde Nar-

ramore. Now, more than 50 years later, we have celebrated our golden wedding anniversary. No wonder we feel a soft spot in our hearts for Jack! Schroon Lake also holds a special place in my heart for it was there that our daughter, Melodie, gave her heart to the Lord. Jack was a great man – a firebrand for Jesus. He touched many, many lives…and I shall be eternally grateful for his godly influence upon my life.

Dr. & Mrs. Clyde Narramore

From the Narramore Christian Foundation in their magazine, "Psychology for Living"

Jack was loved by all the staff and families in Word of Life as well as all the boys and girls who came to the Word of Life Ranch. They called him "Uncle Jack." One letter that was sent by Jonathan Bubar to his brother, Dan, a Word of Life missionary in Hungary, said it all:

Dan, the main reason that I wanted to write is to talk a little about Uncle Jack's Homegoing. Sometimes I sit and listen to people postulate about him, and how he was "just a man" and it really frustrates me deep down inside.

Even though we were expecting this to happen, it is different when it actually happens. I want you to know that I understand how you are probably feeling right now. Uncle Jack was in many ways my hero and yours as well, and it is different when a hero dies. Next to Dad, Jack was the person I admired and respected more than anyone. He really did hold forth the Word of Life. I know that right now you are surrounded by people who knew about Jack, but you grew up around him and really knew him, and he knew you. He prayed for you often. Do you have any idea how many times he came up to me and asked how things were going with you in Hungary? Many!! I was just thinking that maybe you would appreciate a word from someone who understands where you are coming from.

Paul Bubar, Director of the Overseas Division of Word of Life, and the father of Jonathan and Dan, added this note:

This is a staff kid's perspective on Jack and his Homegoing. I don't know if the greater Word of Life family knows how much Jack was loved and how his memory will be cherished by all the staff kids!

One month later, Dan Bubar was taken Home to be with the Lord very suddenly and is now with the Lord and his "Uncle Jack."

We miss Jack, but we know that he is already with the Lord whom he loved and served, and we are looking forward with great anticipation to that day when we will join him and all those who have gone before us.

Mrs. Joni Erickson Tada Joni and Friends

Only eternity will truly reveal the significant impact Jack Wyrtzen's life had upon the world. I have an inside feeling that if we were to measure, or if we would try to count, or if we would try to figure it all out, our calculations would be much like the statistician trying to number the sand on every seashore. Let's just say that his life was like a giant rock dropped in the middle of the ocean whose waves have impacted every continent, most islands, and most peoples of the world. Thousands of people have come to know Jesus Christ as their Savior through the obedience of one man. Jack is one of the top five men whom I have ever had the privilege of knowing. He personally impacted my life month by month more than any other man.

Dr. Wendell Kempton

Association of Baptists for World Evangelism

Jack was a faithful proclaimer of the Gospel. He never gave up, and he never compromised. He has had a glorious welcome in heaven! The last time I saw him we hugged each other and had a brief prayer together. I was deeply moved. I loved him very much in the Lord.

Dr. Billy Graham

The Billy Graham Association

By God's grace we will continue your legacy. Your decision for Christ at nineteen broke the chain of unbelief and began a new commitment to Christ, His holiness and a faith that caused you to repeatedly say, 'I am just as sure of heaven as though I had already been there for a thousand years.' What is the essence of your life? Is it an intense focus to present the Gospel to everyone you met from cab drivers to toll booth collectors, to even your doctors just before your surgery? You were always handing out the story of your conversion, 'A Passport to Heaven.' We will carry this shoe-leather evangelism and seek to live your constant advice, 'Just spend time daily in the Word and in prayer.' Your uncompromising commitment to your convictions, your personal integrity, the fact that you lived what you preached, this consistency is the rich inheritance you leave to us, your family. We will continue 'on the victory side'!

~ The Wyrtzen family letter read at Jack's "Victory Service"

As I sit out here in Colorado, it seems to me there is a big hole back there in the heart of New York State. It is an empty place that no one can ever fill. For me that will always be known as 'Jack's Place.' As you know, Dawson (Dawson Trotman, Founder of the Navigators) and Jack were buddies – kindred spirits. I've thought about that reunion.

And I can understand the joy Jack has in the men raised up by God to carry on the ministry.

Lorne Sanny

The Navigators

Things will be different without Jack around, to be sure, but I am convinced of God's blessing on Word of Life in ways that will make Jack deliriously happy in Glory.

Woodrow Kroll

Back to the Bible

Perhaps one of the most moving stories about the impact of Jack's life comes from a man who is relatively unknown, living in Sarasota, Florida.

Many years ago, Jimmy Johnson was a prisoner in Sing Sing Prison in New York. He had written to seven ministers to see if they would help him. He heard from only one, and that was Jack Wyrtzen. He went on to say that for the next 12 years in prison, Jack either wrote or called him once a month to see how he was doing. With great emotion he said: "Where would I be except for the faithfulness of a man of God like Jack Wyrtzen."

The Apostle Paul wrote in 2 Timothy 4:7-8: *I have fought the good fight, I have finished my course, I have kept the faith: Henceforth there is laid up for me a crown of righteousness, which the Lord, the righteous judge, shall give me at that day: and not to me only, but also to all who have loved his appearing.* He also said in Philippians 1:21: *For me to live is Christ, and to die is gain.*

The "Victory Service" for Jack Wyrtzen lasted three hours and was used of God to influence the lives of thousands of people. His body was laid to rest in the cemetery in Schroon Lake, New York, awaiting the sound of the trumpet.

1 Thessalonians 4:16-17: *For the Lord Himself will descend from heaven with a shout, with the voice of the archangel, and with the trumpet of God. And the dead in Christ will rise first. Then we who are alive and remain shall be caught up together with them in the clouds to meet the Lord in the air. And thus we shall always be with the Lord. Therefore comfort one another with these words.*

The House that Jack (God) Built is not yet complete. Many more rooms are being added for the glory of God – new and fresh visions, more workers, additional countries, more Bible Schools, and more Bible Clubs. It started as a small house, but the Master Planner, the Architect of the House, is constantly adding new things. The story and the history of Word of Life has always been people. In America and all around the world, the facilities of Word of Life are beautiful... but what gives lasting beauty are the people who have been saved and changed through the Word of God... and praise God it will continue as Word of Life continues to "Hold Forth the Word of Life."

If the Lord tarries, only God knows what will be accomplished as the house continues to grow... to God be the glory!

Jack Wyrtzen – 1913-1996

CHAPTER 16

New Owners

*Show Your marvelous lovingkindness by Your right hand,
O You who save those who trust in You. Psalm 17:7*

You know, as the family grows, so must the house. You not only need room for kids, but now it's the grandkids, and soon it will be the great-grandkids. The house just keeps getting bigger – better and stronger all the time. And, so it has been with the ministry of Word of Life.

Few organizations like Word of Life have been able to survive after the Founding Directors stepped aside. However, because of the vision of Jack Wyrtzen and the flexibility of new leadership, Word of Life has succeeded. Jack Wyrtzen always said, "I believe that it is the responsibility of every generation to reach their generation for Christ," and Jack was committed to that not only in life but also in death. There have been changes in Word of Life, and there will be more in the future. Things are different without Jack. Yet, the new leadership is building upon the strong foundation that was established over many years.

In 1982, Jack Wyrtzen and Harry Bollback invited George Theis, who had been in Brazil for almost 20 years, to come back to Schroon Lake to help in the growing ministry within the United States. He served in many capacities as a Co-Director of Word of Life, and in January 1991, he became the Executive Director. The inauguration of George Theis at the Word of Life Inn was a very special occasion with the participation of outstanding leaders from many Christian organizations. Dr. Joseph

Stowell, who was the president of Moody Bible Institute at that time, was the guest speaker.

In many churches or Christian organizations, the first man to succeed as founder often does not succeed, because it is a difficult role to follow. However, to the glory of the Lord, George was able to give the necessary leadership to make some wonderful things happen and all in harmony with the ongoing work of Word of Life.

Jack and Harry continued assisting in the work under the leadership of George Theis. His style of leadership, which was not to come in and change everything overnight, fit well into the work at that time. George had been part of Word of Life for almost 30 years, so he was familiar with the work, as well as working with Jack and Harry.

Many wonderful things were accomplished in the 1990's that gave great growth and stability to Word of Life. The general public was encouraged to see everything moving ahead so well. People knew there had been a change but felt at ease because it all happened so smoothly. It was the same work – just with a new Executive Director. That doesn't mean there weren't any difficulties, but it does mean that since everyone was committed to the ongoing work of the Lord through Word of Life, all the obstacles were overcome. That is what can be accomplished when people are really committed to the Lord and have a sincere desire to see people reached with the Gospel. So many wonderful ministries and churches have been destroyed because people refuse to labor together for the ongoing work of the Lord.

In God's wisdom and timing, He had prepared George Theis to be the next leader of Word of Life. Not only had God prepared George but also his family. George married Joan Robinson in 1959, and God blessed them with three wonderful children... Linda, Steve and Sherri. Linda married Keith Balsley who works on the staff of Word of Life Florida. Steve and Marissol Theis and family went to Word of Life Brazil in 1989, and today Steve ministers with SCORE International in Brazil.

Sherri and her husband, Alejandro Belmar, and family have served with

Word of Life in Cuba, El Salvador, and Spain.

George always had a desire to prepare young men for positions of leadership in the work of the Lord around the world. As Executive Director, he put together a group of young people, called the Impact Team, with whom he would work and travel. While they ministered together in meetings, George would teach them how to do the work. It was similar to what Jack Wyrtzen had done for so many years when he would travel with the Word of Life Quartets. The Lord blessed not only the lives of the many people who were saved through this great outreach, but also in very specific ways the lives of the young men who were discipled and trained in this ministry.

The mission of Word of Life has always been to reach youth with the Gospel of Christ. That mission is carried out by reaching out through evangelism initially and then preparing others to carry on the work through personal discipleship. Before going to Brazil, George was used of God in the first Word of Life Bible Club to touch the life of Joe Jordan. Joe was a young man in that Word of Life Bible Club, and George was his club leader in Lakeland, Florida.

George was also used of the Lord to revive a work that had been started years before by Lou Nicholes. It was a program called Youth Reachout, and through it, groups of young people were organized to go to a mission field for a short term, usually two to four weeks. This outreach grew and was a tool for allowing young people to visit the mission fields of the world. Many of these young people would then attend Word of Life Bible Institute and eventually go back to those countries as missionaries. God used that ministry not only to challenge the young people of the need of worldwide missions, but through these evangelistic teams the Gospel was preached and literally thousands of people were saved around the world.

Youth Reachout was only one part of the Overseas Division, now called International Ministries, which expanded under George's leadership.

Facilities were opened in ten new locations bringing the total number of countries where Word of Life was ministering to 44. The Word of Life Bible Institute experienced growth in the size of their student body which, in turn, created a need to open an extension campus in 1997 at our Word of Life Florida facility. Larger classrooms were soon needed at both the Florida and Schroon Lake campuses.

The plans for the Jack Wyrtzen Center in Schroon Lake and the George Theis Assembly Center in Florida were large projects, and the plans for the construction and the fundraising began under George's leadership.

George Theis was the right man for leading the ministry through these years. He was never an aggressive leader but always a steady influence during the 'new owner phase' of the house through the 1990's. He was a leader who loved the Lord and His Word – a man committed to "Holding Forth the Word of Life."

On August 20, 1999, Joe Jordan became the third Executive Director of Word of Life, taking over the responsibilities of the entire worldwide ministry of Word of Life. Joe and his wife, Melva, had been missionaries with Word of Life in Argentina for 20 years, where they had established wonderful ministries in camping, evangelism, clubs, and a Bible Institute. In 1991, Joe returned to the United States to begin working with George in many capacities. In 1995, working under George's leadership as Executive Director, Joe Jordan became the Director of Word of Life. All this was in preparation for Joe to assume the overall responsibilities as the new leader of Word of Life in 1999.

Joe and Melva have three children, Gracia, Andres, and Debbie. Gracia married Mike Laymon, and they live in Dallas, Texas. Andres is married, and they live in Atlanta, Georgia. Debbie married Kris Stout, the Director of Word of Life International Ministries in Schroon Lake, New York.

Right away, Joe Jordan set a goal to have Word of Life in 100 countries by the year 2010, a program called Target 2010. This was an ambitious goal, but having been a missionary for 20 years in Argentina and seeing the value of the Word of Life ministry overseas, he was committed to reaching this goal for the glory of God. This was not merely a goal to be reached but a heartbeat to see thousands of lives being touched for salvation, dedication, and training.

Joe was a dynamic, strong, and compelling leader. He loved the Word of God and, like George, was committed to maintaining the standards and disciplines that have made Word of Life what it is today.

The new classroom building at the Word of Life Bible Institute in Florida, which was started by George Theis, was finished and officially dedicated by Joe Jordan on February 9, 2001, as The George Theis Assembly Center.

The Jack Wyrtzen Center was completed and inaugurated under the leadership of Joe during the Founder's Bible Conference, May 2003, with Dr. Howard Hendricks as the speaker. It is a wonderful addition that has positioned the Bible Institute in Schroon Lake, New York, for continued growth.

In the late 1990's, the office space at the Headquarters building in Schroon Lake was no longer adequate, and plans were being made to build a new office complex. However, God had another miracle in mind. The public school in Pottersville, New York, was consolidating with other schools in the area, causing their building to become available. This would be a wonderful location since the Bible Institute, Ranch and Family Campground are located in Pottersville. The school district was going to demolish the building at a cost of $150,000. Sensing the leading of the Lord, Joe made an offer for the price that it would have cost for the demolition. The offer was accepted, and the building was purchased. It was actually worth much more, but there were no other buyers for such a building in the area.

In the winter of 2001, a late storm brought a very heavy snow, which caused the roof to collapse at the Pine Pavilion auditorium on Word of Life Island. For over 50 years that building had been used to introduce thousands of campers to Jesus. It was a very special place with many memories. Under the leadership of Joe Jordan, a new Pine Pavilion was built and inaugurated in the summer of 2002. The new Pine Pavilion is almost an exact replica of the original one and continues to build new memories for campers today.

In the face of changing times, Joe Jordan was uncompromising in his stand for the inerrancy of the Word of God and the integrity of Word of Life. Joe was a strong leader who moved ahead for the glory of God and the good of Word of Life.

Some may wonder, what is different at Word of Life?

While all our Directors have had the same spirit that Jack had – no one can replace the kind, generous, loving and caring spirit, the phone calls, memos and letters of encouragement that made Jack, Jack. He had concern for people and their struggles with life. Jack had an understanding heart that could disagree with a person and still keep him as a friend. The Jack Wyrtzen smile made you feel like someone really cared about you and that you were very important. The personal witness of a faithful man of God is gone and can never be replaced. Yet, there is no need to replace it because the new team with new ideas, plans and dreams serves and loves the same God that made Jack, Jack.

Consider for a moment the things that have remained the same – the dedication of an organization to stand true to the Word of God, the commitment to world evangelism and personal discipleship and the desire of the new leadership to see the work of the Lord through Word of Life continue to move ahead all around the world.

The Apostle Paul said in 1 Corinthians 16:9: *For a great and effective door has opened to me...* As a ministry, Word of Life continues to look for open doors and to move through them as the Lord leads.

CHAPTER 17

Até Logo –
Until We Meet Again

In an old family house, there are many memories of all the wonderful days spent there. There are memories surrounding all the hard work that has been accomplished and the friendship and laughter along the way. There are also memories of great family celebrations like birthdays, weddings, and births. And, like all families, there are also memories of the more sober days when loved ones pass from this earth to eternal glory. Jack Wyrtzen, the Founder of Word of Life, went to be with the Lord in 1996, and on July 2, 2014, after a short illness, George Theis who had been the Executive Director of Word of Life International from 1991-1999 went Home to Heaven.

George and Joan began their involvement with Word of Life in the summer of 1956 when George served as the Sports Director on Word of Life Island. A few years later in 1959 when Paul Bubar began the Word of Life Club ministry in Lakeland, Florida, George and Joan became the first Word of Life Club missionaries. Their hearts were tender and open to the Holy Spirit's leading, and in 1962 the Lord called them to move to Brazil as Word of Life missionaries working with Harry Bollback and Harold Reimer in the city of São Paulo. Later, as Word of Life expanded in Brazil, George and his family moved to Recife, in the northeastern part of Brazil, where they opened a new Word of Life Camp in 1973. For twenty years George and Joan served the Lord in Brazil, and the country and the people became very much a part of their hearts. Even after George returned to the United States in 1991 to become the Executive Director of Word of Life, George and Joan returned many times to Brazil to visit the people and the work which they loved so much. It was actually on a trip to Brazil in 2014 when George first became sick. Shortly after he returned to the United States, he passed into the presence of the Lord whom he loved and served so faithfully for many years.

George loved the Word of God, and he studied and read it every day. In addition to loving God's words, he also loved people. He was a faithful witness; always ready to give an answer to lost people for the hope that was in him.

In chapter 16 of this book, much was written about George Theis and his accomplishments as the director of the Word of Life ministry. One of the ways briefly mentioned was his intentional discipling of young men. Many of these young men have grown into great leaders within the ministry of Word of Life.

Several of those men have written testimonies describing the magnitude of George's influence in their lives.

The following is the testimony of Joe Jordan regarding George Theis:

"Nothing is so strong as gentleness. Nothing is so gentle as real strength" – R.W. Sockman. Some have a totally wrong concept of gentleness and meekness. It is important to note that gentleness or meekness is not weakness but rather power under control.

I had the honor and privilege of knowing, being influenced by, and serving with George Theis for over 50 years. He was a man of impeccable integrity and immeasurable influence not only in my life but in countless lives around the world. Seeking to define his life, I define him as a strong and gentle leader. It is important to know that leadership is the ability to influence. There are those who think it as imposing one's will upon another, but it's actually influencing others to follow the will of God.

Gentleness is mentioned in the list of the fruits of the Spirit we find in

Galatians 5:22 and 23. It has been said, "To be Christlike is to be strong and gentle." Truly our identity rests in God's relentless gentleness which is revealed in Jesus Christ. This is seen in the words of the prophet Isaiah: "A bruised reed shall he not break, and the smoking flax shall he not quench: he shall bring forth judgment unto truth." (Isaiah 42:3) Most people would break a weak and useless reed, but not so our Savior.

King David realized the strength and gentleness of our God when he said in his song in 2 Samuel 22:36: "...Thy gentleness hath made me great."

Throughout all my years I not only sensed but also witnessed George's strong and gentle spirit. For me this is what made George a godly and great leader. I first met him as a young teenager when he and Joan started the first Word of Life Bible Club in my hometown of Lakeland, Florida, at the home of Eleanor Sutton. I was immediately drawn to him because he was an athlete. He played college football and held his own on the basketball court.

When I saw him throw a football zipping a spiral for some 40 yards on a line, I said, "Wow! I want to be like that man." At that time through my immature teenage eyes, I could only see his strength. My saddest day in those early years was when on a beach at Treasure Island, Florida, he told our Bible Club that he and Joan felt called to Brazil to start Word of Life Bible Clubs and work with Harry Bollback and Harold Reimer. I was stunned to think that my strong hero would leave our city. It was at that time I saw his gentle spirit as he sought to comfort a group of weeping teenagers.

Warren Wiersbe said, "God doesn't manufacture synthetic heroes; He grows the real thing." In the following years I would personally witness "the real thing" in George's life.

Some years later, after I finished high school and was in my final year of college, I received a letter from George inviting me to join him in Brazil and work with him in the Bible Club program. His invitation was what caused me to begin focusing on South America, and although I did not go to Brazil, God used that invitation in my life to lead my wife, Melva, and me to the neighboring country of Argentina.

After we arrived and started the Word of Life Camp in Argentina, we invited George Theis to be our first camp speaker. It was at our very first campfire service on February 9, 1973, that I again saw his strong and gentle spirit. As a result of that campfire service would be a harvest of leaders to go throughout all South America with the Gospel of Christ. Many have been greatly used by God in the ministry of Word of Life, like Beto and Crystal Tarasiuk, Dan and Silvia Nüesch, Andres and Mirta Fernandez Paz, Norberto and Griselda Gimenez. What a harvest for the Glory of God.

Later when the Lord directed George and Joan to open a camp in Recife, Brazil, I had the privilege of traveling there as a guest speaker. His strong and gentle spirit was evident as he ministered to the Brazilian youth.

A few years later the Lord called George and Joan back to the United States to work with Jack and Harry. Then, to my surprise, in 1989, by God's grace, I was invited to work with George when he became the Executive Director for Word of Life on January 3, 1991. It was not only an honor and privilege to work under his leadership for 8 years, but a tremendous learning experience.

At George's installation service, the title of his message was, "A Turtle on a Fencepost." The main idea was that a turtle can't be on the fencepost through its own effort, so someone had to put it there. George did not rest on his own efforts but on his Almighty God who placed him in this position of leadership. More than ever, I saw this strong and gentle spirit, as God used George to eliminate debt, burn mortgages, build buildings, see thousands come to Christ, and, most importantly, build lives for the Glory of God.

George had the vision to start a singing group called, "The Impact Team," who traveled with him and was involved in serving the Lord and sharing the Gospel. The Lord used the discipleship that occurred during those ministry trips to raise up leaders who have touched the world. Two of those young men, Rich Andrews and Kris Stout, now have leadership roles in the ministry of Word of Life.

Through this strong and gentle leader, many things were accomplished for the Glory of God. Some might ask what his secret was and how he accomplished so much for God's glory. I firmly believe the answer is simple; George feared the Lord and honored His Word. Charles Bridges defined the fear of the Lord in the following way, "It is the affectionate reverence by which the child of God bends himself humbly and carefully to his Father's Word." That is a synopsis of my friend and mentor, George Theis.

In a day when many are looking for stars, the need is great for servants. George was a selfless servant of our Lord Jesus Christ. On the day of my installation as the Executive Director of Word of Life, George quoted the words of a great Gospel song, "How can I say thanks, for the things you have done for me? Things so underserved, yet you gave to prove your love for me." Thank you, George; you are still teaching me through your example. "For God is not unrighteous to forget your work and labor of love, which you have showed toward his name, in that you have ministered to the saints, and do minister." Hebrews 6:10

Joe Jordan became the Executive Director of Word of Life in 1999 and served until 2011. He was used of the Lord in wonderful ways during his tenure.

Rich Andrews wrote the following:

My relationship with George began in November 1991 on "The Sights and Sounds Christmas" Tour. After getting into a little bit of trouble during stage call, George met with me and shared the following advice, "You and I can be the best of friends or the worst of enemies; the choice is up to you."

I'm so grateful that I chose friendship. I travelled with George on the Impact Team from 1992-1998. He and Joan did our marriage counseling, and George spoke at our wedding on December 3, 1994. Over the years his encouragement and advice were steady, and he constantly pushed me to be more and more like Jesus.

Rich Andrews became the Director of Word of Life Florida in 2013 and has been used of the Lord in the great growth of the work under his leadership.

Kris Stout also wrote about the influence George's life had on his own:

When I was a student at the Bible Institute, George's gracious leadership was both inspiring and intriguing to me. So, when the opportunity to travel for a year with George and Joe came up, I jumped at it. George had a way about him that gained the respect of all the young men who traveled with him without being heavy-handed or dictatorial. He allowed us to joke and have fun, yet we always knew where the line was. He offered fatherly advice, or even a rebuke, with a sly grin that would put you at ease and made you feel cared for as a young man.

On many occasions he and Joan would invite one of us to travel with them in their car on the way to our next destination, which normally meant that it was time for a joint counseling session from both of them. My 'counseling' time came when they knew I was serious about a certain young lady, and they wanted to make sure I did things right and was prepared for the road ahead. Their advice was extremely helpful (I've been married to that girl for more than 20 years), but of equal impact was simply the proactive concern they showed for my life, something I have tried to model in my own relationships since then.

Kris Stout became the Vice President of Word of Life International Ministries in 2009 and has done a great job in the growth and outreach of Word of Life around the world.

These are just a few testimonies from men whom George discipled. There are many others who are serving the Lord around the world who would echo these same sentiments.

At George's memorial service in Schroon Lake, Harry Bollback spoke and shared from 2 Timothy 4:7-8. *"I have fought a good fight –* 'A good fight.' *I have finished the course* – 'A good finish.' *Henceforth there is laid up for me a crown of righteousness* – 'A great future.' This was the picture of George Theis. He fought a good fight for the inerrancy of the Word of God. He was always strong and contended for the faith. He kept going strong for the Lord to the very end. He finished well, and now he's enjoying the wonderful, sweet presence of the Lord Jesus Christ."

In Brazil there are two ways to say goodbye: Adieus and Ate´ Logo. 'Adieus' is used when you do not plan to see the person again. However, 'Ate´ Logo' means, until we meet again. To our dear brother, George Theis, we say Ate´ Logo because we will see you again!

What a blessed hope we have in the Lord Jesus Christ.

CHAPTER 18

Remodeling

When you stop to think about it, this Old House has been standing for a long time now. As is the case with all houses, there comes a time for a little remodeling. Since 1940 this house has been standing strong, and in 2011 when Don Lough, Jr. was appointed the Executive Director and later, President and CEO of Word of Life, it was time for some remodeling.

The foundation was checked, and to the glory of God the foundation was found to be as strong as the day it was established. The priority of the leaders at Word of Life has always been to maintain a strong foundation by staying true to the Word of God. The Doctrinal Statement of Word of Life has remained the same and will not change. The Word of Life house is strong and solid on its firm foundation. Remodeling is just a time to update and reconfigure. There are now new names, new faces, new buildings, and new ways of doing things in the 21st Century.

What are some of the new names?

The Ranger Camp is now The Ridge. The Family Campground is now The Pines, and Lakeside at The Pines compliments this facility. Lakeside is the former SonRise Lutheran Camp that was sold to a friend of Word of Life and is now operated by the ministry under a long-term lease agreement. Campers are now called Students. Summer Training Corps (STC) is now Camp Crew. Bible Clubs are now called Youth Ministries. The Overseas Division is now International Ministries. The Super Bowls are now called Reverb. The old shield logo has been replaced with a more modern big "W"... and the list goes on.

There are also new faces as many of the older Board Members have either been promoted to Heaven or retired and have since been replaced. These new men are true servants of the Lord who are just as committed to Word of Life as those who served before them. It is fitting to recognize the contributions and the dedication of these men who knew and served under Jack Wyrtzen, Harry Bollback, George Theis, Joe Jordan and Don Lough, Jr. These were strong men who loved the Lord and Word of Life.

Paul Bubar was a faithful and willing member of the Board for 40 years. In addition to serving on the Board, Paul Bubar was the Founder of Word of Life Bible Clubs (now called Youth Ministries) which is a discipleship program that is now in thousands of churches around the world. He has also served as the Director of the Island, the Inn, the Ranch and our International Ministries division. Paul was a great man, and he and his wife, Shirley, have contributed in a great way to the growth of Word of Life around the world.

Ed Galenkamp was a farmer in New Jersey. He was very interested in the ministry of Word of Life and became great friends with Jack Wyrtzen. Ed was especially interested in reaching children with the Gospel, and his desire to reach children fueled his interest in the Word of Life Ranch. Ed made sure that at the beginning of every summer the petting zoo was stocked with plenty of animals for the campers. He would also drive busloads of children up to camp each summer from Hawthorne Bible Church. Ed and his wife, Catherine, were very generous to missionaries and Word of Life during the 41 years he served on the Board.

Kermit Gehman and his wife, Joyce, were part of Word of Life since the opening days of the Word of Life Island and the purchase of the Inn. Kermit and Joyce supported the missionary outreach of Word of Life around the world, visiting the fields and financially helping many missionaries. Throughout the years, Kermit would provide Jack Wyrtzen with new cars from his automobile agency in Pennsylvania. Kermit was a man of prayer and action and served on the Board for 40 years.

Abe Horst worked in the construction business in Pennsylvania, and he became very interested in and involved in the ministry of Word of Life. His expertise in construction and management was of considerable help to Word of Life. He brought wisdom, suggestions, and leadership to the Board, and he was certainly used by the Lord. He and his wife, Marion, were a great part of Word of Life until the Lord took him Home very suddenly. He faithfully served on the Board for 23 years.

John Janho is a businessman in New Jersey who came to know and love the ministry of Word of Life through his commitment to bring his family to summer camp each year. He and his wife, Florence, became good friends with the leadership at Word of Life, and John was soon asked to join the Board of Directors. He brought a lot of business wisdom and financial help to the ministry. After serving on the Board for many years, John decided he wanted to know more about the Bible, so he took a year off work and came to the Bible Institute as a student. John is a man of God and was a member of the Board for 34 years.

Don Kelso was in the insurance business in Florida where he was led to the Lord by Judge Jim Welch, who would also become a Board member. Don Kelso is the businessman who paid for Joe Jordan to attend camp on the Word of Life Island. It was during that week of camp that Joe accepted Jesus as his Savior. Joe would eventually become the Executive Director of Word of Life. Don Kelso and his wife, Dot, were faithful people who did great things for the Lord, and he served faithfully as a Board member. He eventually left his insurance business and became the Director of the Word of Life Overseas ministry. He was a member of the Board for 30 years.

Bill Price and his wife, Mary Jo, received Jesus Christ as their Savior in Zanesville, Ohio, after hearing Jack Wyrtzen preach. Bill was a businessman who fell in love with the work and ministry of Word of Life. He and Mary Jo have visited almost every country where Word of Life has a ministry, and through their financial generosity much has been accomplished for the Lord. Through the years they have been great encouragers and prayer warriors for all the Directors at Word of Life. Bill and Mary Jo love the Lord Jesus, and they love reaching lost people. Bill served on the Board for 32 years.

Barney Van Dyk was a friend to Ed Galenkamp; they were both from Hawthorne Bible Church in Hawthorne, New Jersey. Right after Jack Wyrtzen got saved, he attended Bible School at their church on Monday nights. Barney had a butcher shop in Patterson, New Jersey, until he and his sons started the Van Dyk Manor in Ridgewood, New Jersey. This retirement village continues to this day. Barney and his wife, Evelyn, loved Word of Life and were generous to many missionaries. Barney truly counted it a privilege to be a Board member, and he served faithfully for 13 years.

Ray Adams was an executive with an oil company who was introduced to Word of Life through his wife, Harriet, a childhood friend of Mary Ann (Wyrtzen) Cox, Jack and Marge Wyrtzen's oldest daughter. Ray served on the Board for more than 40 years and contributed greatly to areas of leadership development and continuity, especially with respect to the process of selecting the future Executive Director/President and CEO of Word of Life. He continues to travel, teaching and training leadership in many international Word of Life locations.

New names, new faces, new ways...

The International Ministries Division at Word of Life has responded to Don's leadership and has formulated a new plan to accomplish their vision of world evangelism. Kris Stout, Vice President of the International Ministries Division, explains Don Lough's vision for reaching the world in this way:

Since Don took over as President and CEO in 2011, one of our primary desires has been 'health before growth'. We need to be spiritually healthy, relationally healthy, and financially healthy all around the world, so to not reproduce something unhealthy. We also believe that if something is truly healthy, it will grow. As a result, we have implemented a number of leadership changes, created new levels of accountability, and improved training and missionary care in various areas for our leaders and missionaries.

We continue to use a 'satellite' ministry model to be our main catalyst for

growth. We are challenging our fields to look at neighboring countries to see how they can begin to have impact there on a regular basis. We are also reinforcing 'Regional Sending Centers' by establishing new Bible Institutes in key areas, such as Central America and Africa. These are now producing new missionaries for their regions and beyond, as our other Bible Institutes continue to do.

Word of Life has been present and has grown heartily in areas that were traditional mission fields for years, namely Latin America and Europe. It is now time for us to sharpen our focus on the areas of greatest potential growth: Africa and Asia. Our new Africa Bible Institute has produced our African missionaries who are heading out to new fields such as Ethiopia and Tanzania. Our Philippine Bible Institute has sent our first missionaries to Indonesia where Indonesian Bible Institute graduates await to assist in the ministry there. Other restricted access countries are also being reached as our Latin and European schools are developing new programs to send young men and women into the strategic parts of the world. Word of Life is also partnering with other organizations to reach into areas that have no Gospel witness. God is raising up a new generation of young leaders through our ministries around the world, and by His grace the future is very bright!

In addition to the new names, new faces and new ways, there are new buildings going up as well. The Bollback Student Life Center is part of a big construction program that Don Lough, Jr., along with the Board of Directors, has focused on. This large building is located on our Bible Institute campus in New York. It contains a kitchen and 600-seat cafeteria that services the Bible Institute students as well as students at Snowcamp and Summer Camp. The building also houses the campus store and student lounges. This new facility opened in the winter of

2017. There is also a new student dormitory, Adirondack Hall, and all the campus dormitories have been remodeled and upgraded. In the fall of 2020, the new Huskies Health and Athletic Center opened. This new athletic complex includes a beautiful new gym, weight and aerobics area and a new synthetic turf soccer field.

There are also physical upgrades and remodeling efforts underway at The Pines (Family Campground) and on the Word of Life Florida campus. These projects are all being completed using funds as they become available as that is the business model Don Lough, Jr. has established.

Perhaps of greater value than the abovementioned changes, which are being accomplished debt free to the glory of God, is the wonderful spirit of fellowship that Don and his wife, Darla, have fostered. Don Lough, Jr. is marked by his warmth and care for people around the world and also for his love, care and consideration for all of the staff. He is truly a great man of God. His love for the Word of God, evangelism and discipleship reinforces the foundation which this great house was built upon.

Someone said that being at Word of Life now is just like it was in the old days when Jack and Harry were here. Praise the Lord! We believe the best days are still ahead as Don Lough, Jr. and the staff continue to stand true to the Word of God and continue to hold forth the Word of Life.

CHAPTER 19

Another Goodbye

This book, first published in 1972, has had several updates, all written by the original author. It was last updated in 2016, and in Harry Bollback's own words, "this will be my last (update)."

In January 2021, the Lord called Harry and his wife, Millie, Home. They died six days apart. Harry was 95, and Millie was 93. They were buried together in the Saratoga National Cemetery.

They lived the latter years of their lives at their home in Pottersville, New York. While the aging process presented many physical challenges, they remained strong in spirit and in their love for the Lord and for each other. Daily they faithfully read the Scriptures and prayed together for their family, friends, staff members and supporters of Word of Life.

The story of Harry Bollback was not the normal tale of a Christian leader. Who would have imagined that an aspiring teenage concert pianist would give up a seemingly great career in music on the concert stage to go to the jungles of Brazil to reach primitive people with the Gospel of Christ?

This Brooklyn, New York teenager, who met Jack Wyrtzen in a youth meeting on a Saturday night, was to find himself at the piano in a jail service the next morning ministering with Jack and the members of a new youth work called Word of Life. This was the beginning of over 50 years of ministry that includes 5 years in the jungles of Brazil, 14 years as Co-Founder and Director of Word of Life Camps and Bible Institute in Brazil along with Harold Reimer, and 21 years as Co-Director of Word of Life with Jack Wyrtzen in the United States.

Harry Bollback was living proof that you never outgive God. Although it seemed like Harry was giving up his music to serve the Lord, the Lord chose to give it back to him as a vehicle to communicate the Gospel of Jesus Christ. Harry wrote and led several musical dramas that toured the country annually, and more than 2 million people attended one or more of these programs that were presented in numerous venues throughout the United States, Canada, and the United Kingdom.

Harry was also an evangelist and a favorite speaker at Word of Life's Youth and Family Camps, events and at the Bible Institute. He had a unique way of sharing Biblical truth that challenged young and old to be all that God desires.

As a young teenager, Millie Bollback had attended a youth camp in the Finger Lakes Region of New York. It was there she dedicated her life in service to the Lord, feeling especially led toward missions. From then on, she planned to go to Bible School to prepare to serve her Savior. After high school, a friend who was working at the Word of Life office in New York City told Millie about a job opening for a receptionist. After an interview, she was offered the position, and in January 1946, she began work at Word of Life. In March of 1946, Millie met Harry Bollback, who had been the pianist for Jack Wyrtzen before World War II started. When he returned from active duty in the Marine Corps, it didn't take long for them to begin to get to know one another.

However, Millie was a woman of integrity, and she wasn't willing to compromise her decision to serve the Lord in missions for anything – even love. Unknown to her, the Holy Spirit was already working in Harry's heart. Later that year and independent of Millie, Harry decided he was ready to fully dedicate his life to the Lord, no matter where He led. The two got engaged in 1947, and after a year at separate Bible Schools (in order to better focus on their studies), they were married on June 12, 1948. Harry and Millie were married for 72 years.

Harry and Millie made a great team – they were the best of friends, and their love for one another was evident to all who knew them. Harry and Millie knew how God had gifted them and used those gifts to support and encourage one another in their pursuit of sharing the Gospel with the nations. Throughout their time both on the field and in the United State, Millie kept things together on the home front while Harry traversed the jungles of Brazil and later traveled for Word of Life around the world. Even while raising four children (Linda, Larry, Elizabeth, and Suely) often alone for significant periods of time – nothing was ever too much for her. She was always proud of her husband and continuously encouraged him to keep going for the Lord and never lose heart. Millie was an incredible example of faith, love, and dedication to the calling of God.

Saying the final goodbye to friends is never easy. Harry and Millie Bollback are certainly missed. Their engaging enthusiasm and love for people and for the ministry of Word of Life caused them to be loved by many who considered them to be their friends. Yet, the story of Word of Life continues as the ministry moves forward.

CHAPTER 20

Changes and New Plans...

It would have been impossible for Jack and Harry to envision all the ways God would continue to use Word of Life in the latter years of their lives and after the Lord called them Home. One of their greatest desires was to see the ministry move forward with the work they began. Their hearts would rejoice to know that the passion they ignited burns brighter than ever in the lives of faithful servants in over 80 countries on 6 continents.

More than 80 years have passed since the founding of Word of Life. The House that God Built has experienced many changes. While some rooms no longer remain, other rooms have been expanded, and new rooms have been added.

2020:

A new initiative called Thrive 2025 was launched with new goals in evangelism and discipleship to reach young people in all 50 states in America and in 100 countries around the world.

The International Headquarters office in New York was sold. The International Ministries and Advancement home office teams moved to the campus of Word of Life Florida, and other home office staff relocated to the Bible Institute campus in New York.

2021:

After much prayer and deliberation, the decision was made to sell the Word of Life Lodge (Inn). The sale was completed in 2022.

2022:

Upgrades were completed at the New York Bible Institute that included the launch of two capital campaigns and other generous gifts allowing the entire campus to be transformed. The construction of the Bollback Student Center, the Huskies Health and Athletic Center, Adirondack Hall dormitory, a new soccer field and the remodeling of all existing facilities provide an inviting environment for students to study the Word of God.

The 75th anniversary of camping was celebrated on Word of Life Island. Some have called it an "island that touches the world", as many who dedicated their lives attending a week or more of camp have served God as missionaries, pastors and leaders who have reached untold thousands with the Gospel.

The faces and many of the methods have changed through the years, but the mission remains the same… reaching youth with the Gospel of Christ and discipling them to reach their generation with the only message that produces life change for the Glory of God! Every year, hundreds of thousands of young people around the world hear this message through the worldwide ministries of Word of Life, and the ripple effect of their transformed lives is having an impact that can only be described as God's hand at work.

In chapter 4 of this book, Harry wrote describing Jack, "He had an explicit and complete trust in his Lord and constantly expected God to do the impossible."

The story of Word of Life is filled with God doing seemingly impossible things through ordinary people. Men and women who stepped out in faith, believing God would do great things, as they were faithful to serve and to trust Him.

...For with God, all things are possible. Mark 10:27b

John Nelson
Executive Assistant to the President

This is the house that under God, Jack built.

You know, however carefully you plan and estimate, it always costs more... the work is never done.

Jack Wyrtzen 1913-1996

The Wyrtzen Family

Jack and Marge
Christmas 1983

George Schilling

Word of Life Boat Ride – "Up-the-Hudson"

From left to right: Bob Moon, Norman Clayton, Harry Bollback, Jack Wyrtzen, Carlton Booth, Horace Davis, Larry McGuill, and Bernie Walters

Jack Frequently Spoke at Pentagon Prayer Breakfasts

Early Radio Days, the Saturday Night Rallies Broadcast Live During the Forties and Fifties

Early Television Days

Madison Square Garden,
New York City

Philadelphia Convention Center

Many Rallies Were Held at the Christian and Missionary Alliance Gospel Tabernacle, New York City

The Eighth Anniversary of Word of Life Hour
was Celebrated at Yankee Stadium in June, 1948

More than 40,000 People Attended the Anniversary Rally

Part of the 1,100 Who Trusted Christ as Savior at the Rally

Jack, Harry and Carlton Booth Traveled to the British Isles
in 1946 for Evangelistic Crusades

Part of the One Thousand Korean Soldiers Who Heard the Gospel
During the Fifteen-Day Crusades in 1972

The Passion Play (1984) and Let Freedom Ring (1976) were Written and Produced by Harry Bollback and Presented on National Television

Early Island Speakers Included Jack Wyrtzen, Harry Bollback, Dick Reed, William Allen Dean, and Dr. Robert T. Ketchum

First Island Camp Staff (Harry and Jack 2nd row center)

From the
101st Cavalry,
Jack Never Lost
His Love
for Horses

Don "Robbie" Robertson
Staff Evangelist

The Brown Swan Club (above)
Became the Word of Life Inn in 1953

Ranch Campers – 1958

Joe Jordan Translates for Jack at Word of Life Argentina

Florida Conference Center

Jack and Harry at Word of Life Canada-Quebec

Word of Life Castle in Germany

Jack and Joan Wyrtzen

Harry and Millie Bollback

George and Joan Theis

Joe and Melva Jordan

Don and Darla Lough

The George Theis Assembly Center – Hudson, Florida

The Harry Bollback Performing Arts Center – Hudson, Florida

Huskies Health and Athletic Center – New York Bible Institute Campus

The Jack Wyrtzen Center – New York Bible Institute Campus

Bollback Student Life Center – New York Bible Institute Campus

Word of Life.